T0326245

Cambridge Elements

Elements in the Gothic
edited by
Dale Townshend
Manchester Metropolitan University
Angela Wright
University of Sheffield

CONTEMPORARY
BODY HORROR

Xavier Aldana Reyes
Manchester Metropolitan University

CAMBRIDGE
UNIVERSITY PRESS

CAMBRIDGE
UNIVERSITY PRESS

Shaftesbury Road, Cambridge CB2 8EA, United Kingdom

One Liberty Plaza, 20th Floor, New York, NY 10006, USA

477 Williamstown Road, Port Melbourne, VIC 3207, Australia

314–321, 3rd Floor, Plot 3, Splendor Forum, Jasola District Centre,
New Delhi – 110025, India

103 Penang Road, #05–06/07, Visioncrest Commercial, Singapore 238467

Cambridge University Press is part of Cambridge University Press & Assessment,
a department of the University of Cambridge.

We share the University's mission to contribute to society through the pursuit of
education, learning and research at the highest international levels of excellence.

www.cambridge.org
Information on this title: www.cambridge.org/9781009565165

DOI: 10.1017/9781009280976

First published 2024

A catalogue record for this publication is available from the British Library

ISBN 978-1-009-56516-5 Hardback
ISBN 978-1-009-28096-9 Paperback
ISSN 2634-8721 (online)
ISSN 2634-8713 (print)

Contemporary Body Horror

Elements in the Gothic

DOI: 10.1017/9781009280976
First published online: October 2024

Xavier Aldana Reyes
Manchester Metropolitan University

Author for correspondence: Xavier Aldana Reyes, X.Aldana-Reyes@mmu.ac.uk

Abstract: 'Body horror', a horror subgenre concerned with transformation, loss of control and the human body's susceptibility to disease, infection and external harm, has moved into the mainstream to become one of the greatest repositories of biopolitical discourse. Put simply, body horror acts out the power flows of modern life, visualising often imperceptible or ignored processes of marginalisation and behavioural policing, and revealing how interrelations between different social spheres (medical, legal, political, educational) produce embodied identity. This book offers the first sustained study of the types of body horror that have been popular in the twenty-first century and centres on the representational and ideological work they carry out. It proposes that, thanks to the progressive vision of feminist, queer and anti-racist practitioners, this important subgenre has expanded its ethical horizons and even found a sense of celebratory liberation in fantastic metamorphoses redolent of contemporary activist movements.

Keywords: gothic, body, horror, biopolitics/necropolitics, metamorphosis

ISBNs: 9781009565165 (HB), 9781009280969 (PB), 9781009280976 (OC)
ISSNs: 2634-8721 (online), 2634-8713 (print)

Contents

1 Body Horror, Then and Now

1.1 History and Context

'Body horror', loosely defined as a subgenre of horror concerned with the maiming, destruction, transformation or grotesque exaggeration of the human body, is not a recent phenomenon. Despite the popular association of body horror with the 1980s, a period that did in fact coin the term and produce the first influential theorisations of spectacular corporeality in horror films, the primary concerns of this subgenre can be traced much further back.[1] First-wave Gothic novels and fin-de-siècle canonical texts, especially Mary Shelley's *Frankenstein* (1818), Robert Louis Stevenson's *Strange Case of Dr Jekyll and Mr Hyde* (1886), Bram Stoker's *Dracula* (1897) and Robert Marsh's *The Beetle* (1897), already delved into many of the concerns that would become the province of body horror – physical difference as a source of abjection, anxieties about contagion and degeneration, and the loss of a stable sense of human identity – and thereby turned the body and mind into concerted loci of fear.[2] And before the narrative techniques of what would eventually come to be marketed as 'horror' in the twentieth century began to formalise in the shape of the Gothic romance and the nineteenth-century penny dreadful, a discourse of exceptionality and caution had already surrounded accounts of monsters and mythical beasts in ancient classical literature and poetry.[3] It is therefore plausible to conceive of the intricacies of body horror as constant and universal, if simultaneously time-sensitive and culturally bound, anxieties that permeate the broader art of terror for entertainment. Worries over beauty, body shape and myriads of other corporeal markers that affect human relations and underpin economic, medical, linguistic and judicial exchanges exist across countries and continents, and prejudices such as ageism, disablism, racism or misogyny are widespread.

The very porosity of body horror means that it customarily bleeds into the wider genre, as social taboos tend to concern bodily boundaries and notions of appropriateness, cleanliness and purity set in opposition to decay, dirt and death.[4] The reveal shock of the corpse at the end of *Psycho* (Alfred Hitchcock, 1960) derives part of its force from the fact that Norman Bates has taxidermised his mother, in contravention of Western interment practices that separate the living from the dead

---

[1] Brophy (1986) is typically seen as the academic inception, not least because the article appeared in a *Screen* issue titled 'Body Horror' also including important research by Barbara Creed and Pete Boss. It is worth pointing out that Brophy's contribution was a reprint of a piece that had first appeared in Australian magazine *Art & Text* in 1983. Although *Screen* did not hyphenate the word, it appeared as 'Body-horror' in both versions of Brophy's article.

[2] See, among others, Halberstam (1995), Hurley (1996), Morgan (2002), Aldana Reyes (2014) and Mulvey-Roberts (2016).

[3] See Cueva (2024).   [4] See, for example, Douglas (2009).

and understand burial as a respectful way of laying the remains of loved ones to rest. Hannibal Lecter, the refined criminal antagonist of Thomas Harris's novels and their successful adaptations, is well known for his cannibalism, an unlawful practice that objectifies human bodies. Mainstream classics such as *The Exorcist* (William Friedkin, 1973) and *Carrie* (Brian De Palma, 1976), not typically considered body horror, cannot help but rely on some of the tropes of the subgenre. Their heroines embody the 'monstrous-feminine' (Creed, 1993: 1–15), whose threatening otherness is defined by amplified female reproductive difference, the expression of which is necessarily corporeal and revels in ejecta like menstrual blood. Due to their connection with the emergence of monster movies and the mad science tradition in cinema, classics like *Frankenstein* (James Whale, 1931), *Doctor X* (Michael Curtiz, 1932) and *Mad Love* (Karl Freund, 1935) are not generally labelled 'body horror' either, despite boasting storylines revolving around corporeal nightmares like corpse reanimation (Figure 1), synthetic flesh experiments and defiant transplantations. Since the very notion of the modern, post-Enlightenment medical monster is steeped in the assignation of 'pathological meanings to certain bodily and behavioural traits' (Smith, 2011: 2), it is fair to suggest that body horror became embedded in the language of cinematic horror to the point of perpetuating eugenic and ableist prejudices. The pervasiveness of

Figure 1 Some classic monster films can be seen as body horror *avant la lettre*.
Source: *Frankenstein*, directed by James Whale (Universal Pictures, 1931)

body horror, as well as the difficulty in delimiting what it defines, means that it has received less attention in Horror Studies than more demarcated subgenres like the slasher, folk horror or zombie films and been theorised more tangentially.[5]

There are good reasons why body horror is linked in the popular imagination with the late twentieth century. Some of its best-known examples were released or published between the end of the 1970s and the early 1990s: the earlier work of David Cronenberg, especially *Shivers* (1975), *Rabid* (1977), *The Brood* (1979), *Scanners* (1981), *Videodrome* (1983), *The Fly* (1986) and *Dead Ringers* (1988); *Alien* (Ridley Scott, 1979) and the art of H. R. Giger; Sam Raimi's *The Evil Dead* (1981) and *Evil Dead II* (1987); *The Thing* (John Carpenter, 1982); Frank Henenlotter's *Basket Case* (1982), *Brain Damage* (1988), *Basket Case 2* (1990) and *Frankenhooker* (1990); *Altered States* (Ken Russell, 1980); *The Stuff* (Larry Cohen, 1985); Peter Jackson's *Bad Taste* (1987) and *Braindead* (1992); Stuart Gordon's *Re-Animator* (1985) and *From Beyond* (1986), which were followed by Brian Yuzna's *Society* (1989) and *Bride of Re-Animator* (1990); *Street Trash* (J. Michael Muro, 1987); Clive Barker's *Hellraiser* (1987), as well as the stories in his *Books of Blood* (1984–1985) and the wider 'splatterpunk' movement they were seen to engender (including fiction by David J. Schow, John Skipp and Craig Spector, Joe R. Lansdale and Shaun Hutson); Japanese cyberpunk classics like *Akira* (Katsuhiro Otomo, 1988), Shinya Tsukamoto's *Tetsuo: The Iron Man* (1989) and *Tetsuo II: Body Hammer* (1992), and *964 Pinocchio* (Shozin Fukui, 1991); and gore films like *Naked Blood* (Hisayasu Satō, 1996) and *Organ* (Kei Fujiwara, 1996). As this by no means exhaustive list shows, body horror was predominantly a visual artistic subgenre, even though novels like Robin Cook's *Coma* (1977), Angela Carter's *The Passion of New Eve* (1977) and *The Bloody Chamber* (1979), Iain Banks's *The Wasp Factory* (1984), Katherine Dunn's *Geek Love* (1989), Dennis Cooper's *Frisk* (1991) and Poppy Z. Brite's *Exquisite Corpse* (1996) trod similar ground. The rise of body horror fiction must also be understood within the market context of the horror paperback boom, which saw novels such as James Herbert's *The Rats* (1974) and *The Fog* (1975) or Gregory A. Douglas's *The Nest* (1980), to name only three, resort to gross, anatomically detailed displays of violence that mirrored the rise of cheap kills in slasher films.

---

[5] Apart from a few articles and chapters, monographs have thus far dealt with broader adjacent genres like 'splatter', 'gore' or the 'gross-out' film; have approached distinct subareas, like the transplantation trope, from a Medical Humanities perspective; or else considered body horror as part of larger studies of the body or biology in the horror genre. The exceptions are Badley (1995; 1996), who explores body horror alongside ghost films and slashers between the mid-1970s and mid-1990s, and Huckvale (2020), who reads body horror alongside existentialist philosophy. At the time of writing, there is no comprehensive history, academic or popular, of the body horror subgenre.

Body horror is partly a child of the golden age of practical effects, prosthetics and animatronics championed by great artists like Rob Bottin, Stan Winston, Rick Baker, Alec Gillis and Tom Savini, who had witnessed human atrocity at close quarters during his time as a combat photographer. Among many other noteworthy events, the 1980s was a decade when horror, and the body horror subgenre in particular, won Oscars for 'Best Makeup' (John Landis's *An American Werewolf in London* in 1981; *The Fly* in 1986 (Figure 2)) and 'Best Visual Effects' (James Cameron's *Aliens* in 1986). It also produced some of the most impressive and limb-cracking cinematic transformations in *The Howling* (Joe Dante, 1981), *An American Werewolf in London* and *The Thing*. Some scenes, like the head explosion in *Scanners* or the chest-bursting scene in *Alien*, are so emblematic that they have been parodied and imitated ever since. The first issue of *Fangoria*, a magazine that became the epitome of gory cinema and special effects during the 1980s, was first published in 1979, boasting a richly illustrated article on Savini's work for *Dawn of the Dead* (George A. Romero, 1978).[6] *Fangoria* would go on to report on, and give cover treatment to, many of the films that today emblematise body horror. Even distinguished magazine *Sight and Sound* devoted part of a full feature on 'Movie Nightmares' to body horror in 1993, an indication that the term had by then travelled beyond

Figure 2 Body horror is associated with special and make-up effects.
Source: *The Fly*, directed by David Cronenberg (Brooksfilms and SLM Production Group, 1986)

---

[6] As Kendrick (2009: 158) notes, *Fangoria* first marketed itself as a fantasy magazine, but by the seventh issue (August 1980) had already narrowed its scope to horror.

Figure 3 Horror had grown visibly more violent and gruesome
by the end of the 1960s.

Source: *Night of the Living Dead*, directed by George A. Romero (Image Ten, 1968)

academic and fan subcultural communities and entered general parlance.[7] As
might be expected, the language in the article highlights the luridness and
visually striking elements of the subgenre.

Body horror's parades of metamorphosis and carnage, and even the idea of
corporeal havoc as anything other than morally unjustifiable, gratuitous and in
bad taste, had been made possible by seismic changes in the 1960s, chief of which
was the weakening and eventual replacement of the American Production Code,
in place since the 1930s, that had prohibited 'brutal killings' from 'being presented in detail' (quoted in Doherty, 1999: 355). The loosening of regulations
issued forth a new era defined by explicitness, the 'New Hollywood', spear-
headed by *Bonnie and Clyde* (Arthur Penn, 1967) and *The Dirty Dozen* (Robert
Aldrich, 1967), both released during 'a breakthrough year for extremely violent
films' (Krämer, 2005: 51). Comparable developments in the UK, Italy, France
and Spain, countries responsible for much of the often independent horror cinema
that flooded theatres during the 1960s and 1970s, heralded the arrival of directors
like Herschell Gordon Lewis, whose colour-saturated *Blood Feast* (1963) has
been hailed as the birth of 'gore', or George A. Romero, whose game-changing
Night of the Living Dead (1968) birthed the cannibal zombie (Figure 3). Films
like Terence Fisher's *The Curse of Frankenstein* (1957) and *Dracula* (1958),
Peeping Tom (Michael Powell, 1960), *Eyes Without a Face* (Georges Franju,
1960), Mario Bava's *Black Sunday* (1960) and *The Whip and the Body* (1963),
Mill of the Stone Women (Giorgio Ferroni, 1960), Riccardo Fredda's *The Horrible*

---

[7] See Williams (1993). The first mention of the term was in 1991, in an article on Arnold
Schwarzenegger, and was applied to describe the short *The Big Shave* (Martin Scorsese, 1967),
a Vietnam allegory, in 1992.

Dr Hichcock (1962) and *The Ghost* (1963) or *Horror Castle* (Antonio Margheriti, 1963) pushed the envelope of what the horror genre could be, increasingly upping the erotic and violent antes and leading to the heady cocktails of nudity and blood typical of the films of Paul Naschy (Jacinto Molina) or the 'horrotica' of Jesús (Jess) Franco and Andrea Bianchi. By the end of the 1970s, horror exuded an aura of transgression; it had become a receptacle for risky material that would have hardly found a footing in more realistic cinema. The bombastic corporeal spectacles of body horror were directly affected by this recent history and by the gradual expectation that horror should be raw and confrontational.

Yet, important as technique and industry were to the honing of body horror on screen, reducing its emergence to a matter of practical innovation, disinhibition and provocation would fail to account for the profound changes that had revolutionised the social landscape between the late 1970s and the 1990s. The most consequential of these was the rise of identity politics that grew out of mid-century social activism and built a shared sense of citizenship that channelled attention into matters of race, gender, sexuality and class, and raised issues of inequality, oppression and repression. Although individual struggles have their own timelines, it is helpful to see the 1960s and 1970s as a period in which the post-1950s civil rights movement, second-wave feminism, post-Stonewall gay liberation movements and New Left activism galvanised into new analytical frameworks that encouraged empathy and the understanding that human bodies are always caught in the crossfires of social processes of valuation and curtailment of freedoms. A good indication that the corporeal begins to be seen as thoroughly constructed by culture and political–legal processes is surely the coining of 'intersectionality' by Kimberlé Crenshaw, a concept intended to shed light on how 'dominant conceptions of discrimination condition us to think about subordination as disadvantage occurring along a single categorical axis' (1989: 140). The writings of Martin Luther King Jr, Betty Friedan, Hélène Cixous, Luce Irigaray, Frantz Fanon, Edward Said, Georges Bataille, Antonio Gramsci and Louis Althusser came to challenge apparently inherent, but in actuality thoroughly artificial and biased, ideas of identity and citizenship and, by extension, the external elements that mark a body as different from the white, patriarchal, monogamous, heterosexual, middle-class and Christian norm. This turn to the inscription of ideological forces onto the body can also be traced in Film and Literature Studies, with, for example, film journal *Cahiers du cinéma* explicitly embracing Marxism from 1968 to 1973 or the publication of Laura Mulvey's article on the male gaze in 1975; the emergence of a string of foundational feminist literary studies by Kate Millett, Ellen Moers, Sandra M. Gilbert and Susan Gubar, and Elaine Showalter; or the appearance of key books on the

Figure 4 Influential philosopher Michel Foucault coined the term
'biopower' in the 1970s.
Source: Bettmann / Contributor / Getty Images

relationship between racism and cinematic representation like Donald Bogle's
Toms, Coons, Mulattoes, Mammies, and Bucks (1973).

Michel Foucault's writings on 'biopower' were crucial in advancing the
notion that, much as Althusser had argued about the complicity between
educational and cultural institutions and the disciplinary nature of the state,
there is a direct correspondence between medical and legal discourses as well as
between expressions of identity and their wider policing and punishment
(Figure 4).[8] Foucault speculated about a gradual shift in the seventeenth century
from the pre-eminent punitive right of the sovereign to exercise power by
'*tak*[*ing*] life or *let*[*ting*] live' (1998: 136, italics in original) towards biopolitical
strategies through which the 'biological came under State control' (2004: 240)
and power was 'exercised at the level of . . . the species, the race, and the large-
scale phenomena of population' (1998: 137). Embedded within this new state of
play was the type of controlling, monitoring, and organising bodies to which the
statistical society is heir. For Foucault, biopower operated by '*foster*[*ing*] life or
disallow[ing] it to the point of death' (138, italics in original), with the right to

---

[8] His famous article 'Ideology and Ideological State Apparatuses (Notes Towards an
Investigation)' was first published in the journal *La Pensée* in 1970 and appeared in English
translation in 1971.

kill only exercised to exterminate perceived threats – for example, as justification for colonial massacres. Achille Mbembe would eventually extend this notion through his work on 'necropolitics', or 'contemporary forms of subjugation of life to the power of death' (2003: 39–40), in his writings on the structures of power in the plantation and the colony. For Foucault, disciplinarian techniques of punishment and control, once represented by institutions of power as instruments of the government, did not vanish, but gradually began to work in tandem with, even become subsumed by, more abstract regulative methods or *'techniques* of power' like social contracts and the normalising, hierarchising and segregationist effects of demographic calculations (1998: 141). In short, we see a move from the exertion of power upon individuals (bodies) to human masses (the body politic). Implicitly, biopower becomes internalised; citizens are ideologically interpellated by biopolitical imperatives and reproduce (or challenge) them in their personal behaviours and judgements. Foucault thus provided the scaffolding upon which countless critiques of the 'normative' would be built. In fact, Robin Wood's seminal piece 'An Introduction to the American Horror Film' (1979: 7–28), responsible for applying the 'return of the (socially) repressed' theory to horror cinema, can be helpfully re-imagined as a continuation of the intellectual advances of the 1970s. Many body horror texts are shot through with analytically disapproving, if not reformist, messages about the position of the body in modern society.

Finally, it is important not to overlook the valence of postmodernism, debates about which characterised the 1980s and foregrounded new artistic forms defined by their 'empirical, chaotic, and heterogenous' qualities (Jameson, 1991: 1). On a superficial level, body horror displays the 'self-awareness' indicative of postmodernity, offering a 'spectacular display' of excessive and curious what-if scenarios sometimes undercut by humour and 'comic transgression', most evident in 'gross-out' scenes that draw attention to special effects, emphasise affect over meaning, and toe the line between the revulsive and the physical excess of slapstick (Grant, 2007: 355). For some critics, like William Paul, horror from the 1970s and 1980s was marked by a 'playfulness' (1994: 423) observable in its narrative beat (a series of horrific numbers close to comedy that had its most direct predecessor in the EC comics of the 1950s) and 'the end of closure' (416) of films like Alfred Hitchcock's emblematic *The Birds* (1963). In its insistence on mixing Bakhtinian explosions of bad taste with deeper considerations of the status and positionality of certain human bodies, body horror also partakes of the melding of high-brow and low-brow orders that is another cognate of postmodernism's irreverence and lack of regard for neatly designated categories. This roguish flirtatiousness is also detectable in body horror's intergeneric tendencies (its absorption and repurposing of elements from science fiction, horror, comedy, melodrama and romance), which offers an explanation for the historical difficulty in demarcating the subgenre.

The plasticity and elasticity of postmodernism translated into conceptions of corporeality, with the self perceived as 'incomplete' and always 'in process' (Sarup, 1996: 47) and identity as fractured. The Western body began disintegrating following challenges to its cohesion from psychoanalysis, which had complicated the relationship between the conscious and the unconscious in the early twentieth century, and then post-structuralism, which revealed corporeality as a process of legibility and medical, legal and cultural inscription that brought to the fore the lack of ownership and control we have over its freedoms and meanings. The body also became ever more metamorphic and polymorphic as subjectivity grew external and accessorial, built upon 'individual hyperconsumption' (Jameson, 2009: 72) in mainstream channels, or else extreme modification in countercultural communities like the Modern Primitivism of the late 1980s. Historical contingencies contributed to the decentring and perceived pliability of the human body, so that we can speak of its unmooring from the sacred sphere and re-rooting into materiality and the promises of biotechnology. Genetic engineering underwent a period of intensification between 1958, the first time DNA was made in a test tube, and 1996, the momentous cloning of Dolly the Sheep (news of which drew on Frankensteinian metaphors), raising fears about replication and forms of genetic selection redolent of eugenics. Patrick Gonder writes of 'a shift in the discourse of embodiment' through which the body became imbued 'with a somatic unconscious, an invisible aspect that governs physical form' (2003: 34). Commensurate milestones in robotics, ranging from sensor technology that gave machines autonomy of movement (1949) to the first pioneering use of AI (early 1970s), renewed anxieties over the mechanic replacement of the human. The same commingling of technology and flesh was responsible for the rise of transhumanism (a term coined as early as 1957) and an interest in the feminist possibilities of the cyborgian body.[9] The detonation of the atomic bomb and subsequent nuclear destruction of Hiroshima and Nagasaki in 1945, commonly taken as the beginning of the Atomic Age, brought worldwide attention to the effects of radiation on the human body, its external branding of cellular damage. The AIDS crisis, compounded by the media focus on tell-tale lesions like Kaposi's sarcoma, once again placed the spotlight on the exteriorisation of the internal life of the body. Advances in science yielded the first contraceptive pill, issuing forth a new age of sexual freedom with repercussions beyond the strictly reproductive. By the late 1980s, the 'interrogation of cultural, historical, and philosophical constructions of

---

[9] See Huxley (1957: 13–17) and Haraway (1985).

corporality' had become such that critics like Cecile Lindsay began talking about a corpus of 'Body Criticism' (1991: 33). Body horror is a symptom of these historical, medical, technological and sociopolitical shifts, if not its direct offspring.

1.2 From Anatomy to the Body Politic

As I have argued elsewhere, all horror could be said to be 'biological' to some degree by dint of the fact that it seeks to elicit pleasurable negative emotions on viewers or readers – that is, it is entertainment that evokes dread, suspense or shock, states of mind and body that humans shun in real life due to their possible detrimental effects (Aldana Reyes, 2022: 107). Such a statement is concerned with the rudimentary operations of the horror experience, rather than with the thematics of given texts, which might be subdivided according to unique patterns and subgenres like ecohorror or folk horror. Body horror is biological in a much more self-evident manner: it deals straightforwardly and narratively with human biology, which is not to say that it is only interested in the so-called natural body. In this respect, the main propositions I want to put forward in this book are: (1) that body horror is a recurring relational subgenre that evolves alongside and in response to ever-changing corporeal norms and directives, making visible normalised processes of biopolitical surveillance and regulation, and thus calling attention to corporeal privileges and social injustices; (2) that body horror locates fear within the body, not just its vulnerability to attack and harm, as most horror does, but also our sense of subjective unity, identity and civil rights; (3) that the type of peril body horror characters face is one that leads to a process of objectification or dehumanisation of the person or else a dissipation and even loss of the 'self'; and, finally, (4) that contemporary body horror increasingly includes a reconstitutive phase that is ethically under-pinned and revelatory, sometimes organised around the integration of the 'other' into the 'self' or of the individual subject into a community.

In his excellent assessment of body horror's physiological underpinnings, biologist Ronald Allan López Cruz surveyed the core human anxieties that find a voice in the subgenre's 'manipulation and warping of the normal state of bodily form and function', or 'the way it goes against what is considered normal anatomy and function in biological species (not limited to human)': 'monstrous hybrids; mutations and diseases that are manifested as physical and behavioural deterioration; metamorphosis; and zombification' (2012: 161–62). Hybridity is frightening not only because it bulldozes taxonomic exactitude but also because in the animal world species are defined by interbreeding and the procreative passing on of genes; individuals from different species are prevented from

Figure 5 Species indeterminism generates a sense of impurity
and instability in body horror.
Source: *The Thing*, directed by John Carpenter (The Turman-Foster Company, 1982)

mating by their physical disposition because the process would lead to infertile
or 'evolutionary dead-ends' (162).[10] Categorical confusion is also advocated by
metamorphosis, which in the natural world is 'adaptive' (163) insofar as it
affords more varied food resources and removes competition for them between
youngsters and adults. In body horror, these metamorphoses are rarely prag-
matic or strictly beneficial, something that distinguishes them from transformations in fantasy or mythical texts. Likewise, mutations, although necessary for
evolutionary purposes, can be the source of bodily and psychological disorders –
affecting symmetry, an indicator of health and prized characteristic in the
animal kingdom – and lead 'to severe physical and behavioural aberrations'
(164). In body horror, our usually stable cellular footing is thrown into turmoil.
Anatomies become flexible, permeable and in flux, and therefore unreliable,
prone to growing impossible, dangerous or impractical limbs and organs that
confuse and pollute species purity (Figure 5). Our lives involve a sizable
number of exercises designed to keep our body in check, from the identification
of threatening conditions to the treatment of disease and the maintenance of
enough cleanliness to prevent ailments. Much of body horror therefore relishes
the sick body, and its connotations with deterioration and death, and in some
cases contagion, as is evident from films like *Cabin Fever* (Eli Roth, 2002),
Thanatomorphose (Éric Falardeau, 2012), *Contracted* (Eric England, 2013) or

---

[10] This is the case of the mule, which is an infertile hybrid.

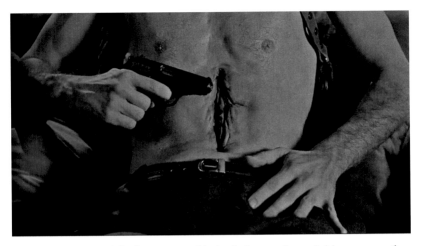

Figure 6 Corporeal limits are tested in body horror through bizarre growths, transformations and hallucinations.

Source: *Videodrome*, directed by David Cronenberg (Filmplan International and Canadian Film Development Corporation, 1983)

The Beach House (Jeffrey A. Brown, 2019) and Naben Ruthnum's novel *Helpmeet* (2022). Finally, the zombie, as a literal walking corpse, represents the utmost in abjection, signifying the final disintegration of the flesh, the process whereby the living organism becomes waste (López Cruz, 2012: 166).[11] Put simply, body horror is biology run amok, messy corporeality refusing to be boxed in or contained, the return of the embarrassing, disobedient or unsocialised body.

Categorical transgressions of bodily signification are inherent to the ingrained unruliness of body horror. In modern horror, the distance between hero and monster, self and other, the external and the internal disappears. As Andrew Tudor remarked of films like *Alien*, *The Exorcist*, *Rabid* and *Videodrome*, traditional sex boundaries are combined into 'a threatening composite' in the bodies of their protagonists, an act that necessarily undermines their supposed 'natural' limits (1993: 31). I would add that such bodies are also fascinating (Kane's incubation and birthing of the chestburster, Regan's androgynous appearance, Rose's empowering armpit phallus, Max's abdominal gash (Figure 6)) and prompt an interrogation of the identities defined by the markers they deliberately trouble and repurpose. It could be countered that the liberating elements of such texts are short-lived and even doomed to fail, as in many cases

---

[11] Philosopher Julia Kristeva famously claimed that the 'corpse' is 'the utmost of abjection' (1982: 4).

the strange conversions, hybridisations and transfigurations are lethal to intra-diegetic characters, but this does not mean that their propositions need to be conceived as detrimental, less innovative or unenjoyable. Besides, body horror texts tend to create sympathy for their protagonists and resist endings that merely return us to a cleansed *status quo*. If threatening agents are destroyed, the possibility of their return is imminent and their sullying of corporeal integrity hard to shake off. The othering of body horror does not operate as a reifying conservative defilement rite but as a spanner in the works of assumptions about biology and its accretions of cultural meaning.

Another way of putting this is that when body horror presents us with corporeal doubt, its questioning extends to the body politic. After all, as Mary Douglas (after Marcel Mauss) proposed, 'the human body is always treated as an image of society' and 'there can be no natural way of considering the body that does not involve at the same time a social dimension' (1978: 78). While Tudor, in the 1990s, read these challenges to 'religion, political organizations, science, commercial corporations, the police' as an indication that '[f]ormerly authoritative institutions' no longer command respect for individuals whose contemporary social lives were marked by 'disorder and incoherence' (1993: 39), the view from the 2020s reveals that body horror is and always has been sceptical of monolithic views on the body. Indeed, body horror shows how the body has always operated as a readable text under public scrutiny and enforced inscription, and how subjectivity is the result of processes of legibility and knowability. Embodiment and desire are enmeshed within, and produced by, representational, symbolic and linguistic systems themselves shaped by histories of power and their resulting inequalities (Foster, 2022: 3), as well as the medical and juridical categories used to understand and differentiate people psychologically and physically. Just as biology only accounts for some aspects of embodiment, the 'body' is now theorised as a discursive composite, a point of convergence for various forms of experience and sociopolitical projection. In Section 2 of this book, I show body horror to be particularly fascinated with the vulnerabilities generated by biopolitical and necropolitical exchanges, from the treatment of despotic characters and corporations that dehumanise others to the blurring and even erosion of the human mobilised by biotechnological dystopias.

Unlike the slasher, with which body horror was lumped together in the past owing to their common interest in the destruction of the body and its fragility, the 'horror' in body horror is corporeal in existential and interrelational ways. If slashers are about predation, cat-and-mouse games of survival, body horror is about the chaos of life, the impossibility of freedom and uniqueness, the erasure of distinctions between the material and the technological, and the penetration of science into all aspects of our everyday lives. This point does not intend to comparatively derail or belittle the power of destruction and confrontation. As Mark Steven argues of 'splatter', violence and gore do themselves act to render visible 'what capital is doing to all of us, all of the time – ... how predators are consuming our life-substances; ... how we are gravely vulnerable against the machinery of production and the matrices of exchange; ... how, as participants of an internecine conflict, our lives are always already precarious' (2017: 13). The modern body and its interpellation by the dictates and whims of late capitalism certainly has a sizeable impact on the kind of corporeal fantasies that define body horror, and therefore, the cultural and social concerns they latch on to reflect back and deconstruct. Fears of consumerist culture are all too evident in films such as *The Blob* (Charles Russell, 1988) and *The Stuff*, and *Society* is a gruesome indictment of economic privilege. Fredric Jameson's assessment that postmodernity announces the '"death" of the subject itself – the end of the autonomous monad or ego or individual' (1991: 15) caused by the decentring threat of an awareness of the economic, legal and biomedical discourses that come together to fabricate our sense of ourselves and the limits of our behaviours has to be counteracted by the rise of 'the culture of the image' (2009: 111), in which personality is constructed through acquisition, adornment and modification. A paradox emerges: we seek to counteract the flattening and demystification of the body by investing it with a meaningfulness and uniqueness derived from systems that absorb and assimilate difference by selling it back as markers of alterity. Body horror is attuned to these exchanges, which it can metaphorise (Figure 7).

Body horror engages more than a critique of existing structures of power and order; it can stimulate fictional journeys (for both characters and viewers or readers) between the self and the other, effectively confusing, blurring and merging these concepts and erecting a new palimpsest in their stead. While earlier body horror presented modified bodies with an initial excitement ultim-ately undercut by caution or fear, contemporary body horror is more interested in the liberatory and speculative possibilities of the shared kinship intrinsic to symbiotic bonds. Body horror is perhaps less visionary and optimistic about the overall ability of its 'mutants' to exist in the current world, to which they pose a threat. In epitomising this opposition, though, body horror does not re-establish binaries but questions the constructed barriers between healthy, acceptable and 'valuable' bodies and their abjected counterparts, including the discriminatory rhetoric used in social processes of subjection and systemic inequality. It applies pressure on the constructed nature of the 'normative' body, and stages awakenings provided by the moral and psychological changes that accompany physical alterations. It turns horror's critical eye inwards and asks viewers to parse their own engagement with and involvement in processes of

Figure 7 Films like *Society*, where a wealthy elite species absorbs the bodies of the disadvantaged, lampoon socioeconomic inequalities.

Source: *Society*, directed by Brian Yuzna (Wild Street Pictures and Society Productions, 1989)

differentiation. It is perhaps a truism that our sense of self is fashioned through comparison and distancing from that which we recognise as different due to contrasting values, aesthetic or other subjective parameters. Body horror proposes a state of vacillation between the self and the other, advocating for the upholding of a third 'self–other' that echoes post-millennial trends like the rise of the sympathetic monster in the works of Tim Burton, Guillermo del Toro and Stephenie Meyer (Figure 8).[12] The incorporation of the other, oftentimes of a feared nightmare, can lead to self-understanding and personal growth in an echo of the 'non-human becomings' that post-structuralist philosophers Gilles Deleuze and Félix Guattari theorised as reciprocal zones of creation (2003: 168–74) as well as of collective action. Section 3 illustrates how body horror can enable forms of rewriting and ideological resistance.

The biological and metamorphic constants that eventually granted body horror the status of distinct subgenre have logically tended to dominate discussions of its value and remit, as well as guided the direction of research into its main artistic exponents. Without seeking to underplay the crucial and very

---

[12] I want to acknowledge here the influence of William Beard's research on David Cronenberg and his use of the 'Other-self', or 'the otherness [that] is actually inherent in the self, only latent and buried' (1994: 166), upon which my own 'self–other' builds. My appropriation places the 'self' before the 'other' to emphasise the process of discovery that prompts a new sense of subjectivity. Unlike Beard, I also think the 'self–other' is a progressive and therapeutic figure.

Figure 8 Body horror's 'self–other' is in dialogue with sympathetic monsters
like the Amphibian Man in *The Shape of Water.*

Source: *The Shape of Water*, directed by Guillermo del Toro (Double Dare You and TSG
Entertainment, 2017)

timely debates that body horror has contributed to and continues to reflect, one
of this book's aims is to extend the general meaning of the term to avoid
a potential conceptual cul-de-sac: its reduction to a distorting mirror of society
or, even worse, an irrelevant and démodé carnivalesque attraction. Body horror
has transformative potential; it can actively encourage empathy for others and
change in oneself. The intention here is not to expand body horror's purview for
the sake of maximising research in this area, though that would be a welcome
corollary, and even less to guard or regulate the application and uses of the term.
Instead, my contention is that the scope of what body horror designates must be
broadened to encompass new contemporary manifestations that, due to their
allegiance to other (sub)generic or thematic strands, may not be readily associated with the 'body horror' rubric, such as some strands of feminist, queer and
Black horror. Utilising the vocabulary and tools of body horror can open up new
avenues of thought that complement and enhance feminist, sexually unprejudiced, trans-inclusive and anti-racist approaches. Body horror is implicitly,
sometimes even explicitly, underpinned by critical interventions in Body
Studies, which comprise research into how biopower moulds perceptions of
gender, race, age, class, beauty and illness, and how corporeality is invested
with significance more generally. In short, our conception of body horror must
grow to embrace the concerns of the subgenre in its present state, as it builds on
its history to capture new timely sociopolitical debates. But what does this new
body horror look like, and why has it become so popular and prevalent?

1.3 Contemporary Body Horror

Of the various theories about the workings and nature of horror, the most influential have posited as the genre's primary indicator the interstitiality of the 'monster', the categorical and taxonomic disruption its presence supposes to the intradiegetic world of characters and the natural laws that govern it (Carroll, 1990: 16).[13] In my own work (Aldana Reyes, 2016: 49–54), I have made a case for the desirability of taking a parallel route that considers the wider experience of corporeal and psychological 'threat' as the hallmark of horror. This involves taking monsters as instantiations of that threat, rather than as the genre's defining trait, given these creatures also often appear in non-horrific texts like children's cartoons or space operas. The approach has the benefit of accounting for films where the human monster is largely *in absentia* or extended into autonomous machineries of punishment. It also accounts for texts that have traditionally fallen in the spaces between the thriller and horror, and is in consonance with the application of evolutionary psychology to readings of the appeal and ludic benefits of recreational fear.[14] One of its main premises is that the horror genre places at least some of its characters, typically the protagonists, in dangerous or life-threatening situations that may be experienced, by extension and at a remove, by readers or viewers.[15] The horror apparatus operates through a complex process that creates an investment in the well-being of those assailed by forces challenging them or wishing them harm. In canonical accounts of horror, agents of fear are scary, abjected 'others', 'disturbances of the natural order' that have to be expelled or destroyed (Carroll, 1990: 16).

My theory of body horror introduces an element of importance to its contemporary reframing: the source of threat, although sometimes initially external or parasitic, eventually manifests within, transforming the essence of the self and/ or fundamentally disrupting its integrity. Metamorphic contemporary body horror needs to be re-envisioned as genuinely committed to portraying social injustices because it both creates a strong alliance between literal intradiegetic victims and the experience of discrimination, and because it grounds such tensions in the self. Body horror's typical movements between self and other, at times leading to incorporation or lack of dissolution, create a fictional engagement between abjected 'other' and ostensibly 'normal' self that reveals the arbitrary construction of the normative body. In turning our bodies into

---

[13] This is also Robin Wood's aforementioned foundational position.

[14] The similarities between the mechanics of horror and the thriller are such that, in some cases, both genres are conflated and their emotional primers studied together, as in Hanich (2010). For studies of horror premised on evolutionary psychology, see Clasen (2017).

[15] This is not tantamount to suggesting that viewers or readers are always aligned with the victims or have to identify with them.

extraneous, ungovernable forces, we are not just confronted with radical differ-ence but encouraged to understand it as a fundamental part of ourselves, accept and even assimilate it. Adam Lowenstein writes of how 'modern horror's minority vocabulary' takes exception to the presumptions that the genre 'thriv[es] negatively on otherness' and that texts in the twenty-first century have helped 'acknowledg[e] actual minority experience' 'as real pain rather than just paranoid fantasy' (2022: 158). Transcending the discourse upon which 'othering' is based requires us to contemplate the fact that we too are capable of monstrous behaviour (3). Body horror takes one step further by proposing that this state of affairs is not exceptional (we 'could' be prejudiced in our acts) but a part of everyday life and constitutive of subjectivity (we 'are' prejudiced in our acts). Such a statement is not tantamount to suggesting that we are intrinsically 'horrible', but a reminder that monstrosity is an acquired trait dependent on external perception. To a greater extent than ever before, contem-porary texts configure monstrosity as a moral or ethical flaw, proffered by greed, lack of compassion or selfishness, and spurn the ableist, spectacular discourse that once equated 'evil' with physical grotesqueries and neurodiversity. This reframing of exceptional bodies, habitually the main selling point of the horror film, riffs off concurrent developments in cinema, such as the wave of new horror films in the 2010s and 2020s that privileged arthouse techniques, slower paces and psychological tableaux derived from the melodrama over edge-of-chair shock effects and gore.

The Orphanage (J. A. Bayona, 2007), Jennifer Kent's *The Babadook* (2014) and *The Nightingale* (2018), Ari Aster's *Hereditary* (2018) and *Midsommar* (2019), *Saint Maud* (Rose Glass, 2019), *Relic* (Natalie Erika James, 2020), *Censor* (Prano Bailey-Bond, 2021), *Men* (Alex Garland, 2022), *Smile* (Parker Finn, 2022) and *Talk to Me* (Danny and Michael Philippou, 2022), to name only some of the most well-known examples, have centred trauma and grief as major catalysts of the horror experience. Negative emotions are corporeally and psychologically inscribed, with traditional external monsters morphing into intrusive, internal hallucinations, and hauntings migrating from mansions and 'terrible places' into the minds of protagonists.[16] In contemporary horror, the threat is personal and latent, even when the damage is generated by the actions of others. Body horror has adopted the language and discourse of trauma and displays the correspondence between mind and body it takes as a given, going as far as to propose that physical alterations – a correlate of underlying mental processes – are not just transformative but sometimes terminal. In films like *Black Swan* (Darren Aronofsky, 2011) and *Hatching* (Hanna Bergholm, 2022),

---

[16] For more on this crucial trend, see Dymond (2022) and Laine (2023).

Figure 9 Ambiguous endings force viewers to think about the role of pain and transformation in body horror.
Source: *Black Swan*, directed by Darren Aronofsky (Cross Creek Pictures, 2011)

ontological transvaluations are irreversible and whether endings are read as positive or progressive (or indeed as factual, rather than imagined or dreamed) depends on our teleological expectations (Figure 9). In some texts, characters may be destroyed by the process of change, but their tragedies take issue with and reject the contexts in which protagonists exist. Influenced by the individualistic turn I mentioned earlier and invested in the upending of the *status quo* as arbiter of taste and decorum, much of contemporary body horror is fundamentally anti-conservative and anti-establishment. The vocabulary of the subgenre is useful in exposing the regulation and disciplining of the body, as well as the mechanisms of surveillance and observation it is subjected to and entangled with.

The evolution of body horror's social consciousness has extended its thematic remit and made it more generically impure. What was once perceived to be excessive graphicness and extremity has moved into the mainstream, as explicitness in streaming television has grown more common. In this book, I cast my net wide, considering both the speculative metamorphic fancies of novels like Rachel Yoder's *Nightbitch* (2021) and Julia Armfield's *Our Wives Under the Sea* (2022) and David Cronenberg's film *Crimes of the Future* (2022), as well as those texts where tyrannical or necropolitical power renders the body a mere object or commodity, whether in 'torture porn' entries like *Saw* (2004) and *Hostel* (2005) or in films that present people as exclusive meals or containers of prized organs. I also consider the importance of contagion, responsible for reanimating the zombie apocalypse narrative, a trope that speaks to both enduring fears about parasitism and recent anxieties about global pandemics, populism and the exploitative extraction of labour by transnational corporations. The free flow and immediacy of digital life relies on a technology that has the capacity to alter human life and labour beyond recognition, as the disastrous broadcast signals in novels like Stephen King's *Cell* (2006) and Jeremy Robert Johnson's *The Loop* (2021) remind us. Contemporary body horror also deals with the darker side of transhumanism. The legacy of cyberpunk on body horror is evident, but the subgenre is shot through with a modern sensibility marred by climate change and the data harvesting scandals that have punctuated the early twenty-first century – a greater awareness of online footprints and of what has come to be termed 'platform capitalism' (Srnicek, 2017) and 'surveillance capitalism' (Zuboff, 2019).

The logic of contemporary body horror, the tapestry of corporeal nightmares it presents, betrays the specifics of our relationship to our own bodies. This relationship is an extension and elaboration of twentieth-century repositionings that themselves sprung from the materialism and anthropocentric viewpoint on the rise since the seventeenth century, when the Renaissance directed its dissecting scalpels and epistemological curiosity towards human anatomy.[17] Our unique connection to corporeality manifests in challenges to the once generally accepted sacredness of the body, belief in a higher spiritual afterlife, the decline of faith and religion in favour of science and reason, and the desacralisation of public spaces.[18] The body has become more factual and all-encompassing than ever before, a carnal medium able to convey messages (through fashion or accessorising), a fluid canvas whose surface is susceptible to creative manipulation (tattooing, bod mod), a genetic file to be unwrapped, pored over and mapped out at near-atomic scales (inherited traits, cellular immunotherapy, nanotechnology). Traditional notions of the grotesque that historically placed the body as the 'lower' end of the human subject and the mind (and soul) as the 'higher' were disturbed once cognitivism and neuroscience made distinct divisions between the two untenable. Representational consequences are appreciable in twenty-first-century cultural productions, perhaps most strikingly is the inclusion of histrionic vomiting scenes (Figure 10) that would have once been the preserve of horror, slapstick and their mutant lovechild, 'splatstick', in highbrow films like *Triangle of Sadness* (Ruben Östlund's, 2022), *Sick of Myself* (Kristoffer Borgli, 2022) or *Babylon* (Damien Chazelle, 2022). Such emetic concessions indicate how physiological motifs assist film-makers in granting their works the gritty realism of life – far from pristine perfection and full of somatic inconveniences (Balanescu, 2023) – while pointing to the taming and normalisation of the peripheral world of abjection.

The body remains a battleground due to the fact that it is intersected by a number of social and legal powers that stand outside the grasp of the individual. Groups and communities whose shared physical or biological traits are subject to

---

[17] See Sawday (1996).
[18] This is a massive and complex topic. For an overview, see Taylor (2007).

Figure 10 The upsurge of grotesque vomiting sprees in high-brow cinema signals a shift in contemporary sensibilities.

Source: *Triangle of Sadness*, directed by Ruben Östlund (Imperative Entertainment, 2022)

prejudice or external scrutiny have turned to body horror in greater numbers because it offers a language through which to combat the disciplining rhetoric that seeks to establish jurisdiction over our freedoms and actions. It is a tragic coincidence that the Roe v. Wade ruling, a landmark 1973 case that made abortion legal in the US, was overturned in an equally seismic decision in June 2022 (Figure 11), less than three months before the premiere of the fifth season of *The Handmaid's Tale* (2017–). Based on the 1985 novel by Margaret Atwood, the series imagines a near-future dystopia in which the wombs of the few fertile women left in the US become the coveted possessions of a refreshed totalitarian patriarchy. The anthology film *Give Me an A* (2022), directed by sixteen female directors in response to the overruling, provides proof that horror is politically engaged and does not take long to process major social changes. For self-explanatory reasons, many of the film's segments, like 'The Voiceless' (directed by Megan Swetlow), resort to metaphorical body horror (women's mouths magically glue shut after news of the ruling spread through social media) in their indictment of a decision taken for ostensibly democratic purposes but which has the effects of silencing a majority and compromising their bodily autonomy.[19] As Section 3 demonstrates, feminism has latched on to body horror in order to rethink female bodies and desires in activist ways. Similar treatments can be observed in texts from LGBTQIA+ artists, with trans writers in particular recuperating the subgenre and infusing it with a confrontational power that bolsters representation and speaks to the experience of discrimination and erasure.

---

[19] An unconnected horror fiction anthology, Roxie Voorhees and Nico Bell's *Mine: An Anthology of Body Autonomy Horror*, was also published that year with the intention to 'fight back', as indicated in its dedication page.

Figure 11 The overturning of Roe v. Wade provoked an immediate public
backlash that included body horror cultural responses.

Source: Yuki Iwamura / Contributor / AFP / Getty Images

Corporeality in such texts is a fluid and fraught space, its gendered reality and
plurality of meanings re-asserted in view of external acts of epistemological
violence seeking to contest its reality. Finally, Black horror, albeit a broader
category that has also found tropes like 'hauntings' particularly fruitful, has
turned to body horror for its ability to concretise the complex interactions between
the body and the political. Films by directors like Jordan Peele and Nia DaCosta
explore Black experiences from a thoroughly embodied perspective that takes in
its stride systemic inequality and the betrayals of white liberalism. Indigenous
artists like Stephen Graham Jones, with the award-winning novel *The Only Good
Indians* (2020), or Jeff Barnaby, with the film *Blood Quantum* (2019), are
likewise rethinking the horror tradition, telling stories about communities that
had once been portrayed only as abject other or magical/mystical stereotypes.

The focus in this book does not exhaust the permutations and prospective
cultural work carried out by body horror. The emphasis is solidly placed on
areas that have gained traction and artistic mass over the first two and a half
decades of the twenty-first century, a time in which climate change and global
warming have also inspired subgenres like 'cli-fi' (climate fiction).[20] Some of
the texts in this branch of speculative fiction have remodelled the unnameable

---

[20] See the essays in Goodbody and Johns-Putra (2018). Like all subgenres, cli-fi existed before the
twenty-first century but intensified following the climate crisis awakening of the 2010s.

creatures of the Weird, popularised by H. P. Lovecraft in the early twentieth century, to tackle Anthropocene guilt and condemn the impacts of human activity on the ravaging of non-human animals and their habitats.[21] Perhaps the best case in point is Jeff VanderMeer's *Southern Reach Trilogy* (2014), where Area X, a part of the United States whose flora and fauna have been genetically modified by an extraterrestrial life force, is a blatant analogy for the effects of industrialisation on natural biospheres. While this book references some relevant texts, this is a rich subarea of studies where body horror is hybridising with the Weird at an overwhelming pace. I therefore limit my readings to the appositeness of body horror to the types of global pandemic horrors that anticipated the Covid-19 years (2020–2023). Geopolitical surveillance and crippling isolation are not exclusive to the zombie apocalypse narrative and have been amplified by the intensification of internet usage and the arrival of social media (Aldana Reyes 2023: 342–45). As Marc Olivier notes, the world of the 'postdigital' pulls away from the early fascination of digital media as immaterial and puts forward an entanglement of the human and the non-human that endows the virtual with physical presence (2021: 326). *Black Mirror* (2011–) and the *Years and Years* (2019) miniseries, among many other exponents of dark science fiction, have seen in body horror a shorthand for the (inter)dependence of corporeality and technology. Once again, as definitive and epochal as many of these texts are, there is no space for all of them here. My inferences and postulates on body horror are generalisable, but they cannot possibly paint a complete picture. One of the difficulties of theorising contemporary horror is that it is tough to pick apart; it has become one more main artery in the cultural bloodstream, rather than a niche tributary.

The rise of body horror cannot be separated from the sea change that the wider genre has undergone in the twenty-first century. By the mid-2010s, horror had overcome the exploitative prejudices it had been unfairly accruing over decades of association with pulp, skin-deep entertainment. Genre fans have always known better, and modern artists, many of them coming of age during the 1970s and 1980s, are demonstrating that horror can do more than reflect nostalgia for those decades. It can rethink tropes and subgenres that grew popular in different contexts to tell stories concerned with contemporary notions of subjectivity, control, liberation and transformation. In many of the texts under investigation, the somewhat lone figure of the consumerist individual, typical of the late twentieth century, transmutes into more empathetic collectivist entities aware of economic and social privileges, alert to discrimination and firm in their commitment to meaningful

---

[21] For a definition of the Anthropocene and its engagement with the Gothic tradition, see the essays in Edwards et al. (2022).

change and diversity. The growing number of new voices from groups that had previously struggled to gain access to industries long dominated by white, heterosexual, cisgender men has been crucial in driving this transformation, providing original angles and narratives that shake the foundations of the very construction of horror due to their focalisation – who is scared of what and why. These are creators who know the genre well and are cognisant that its structures still have a lot to offer because their motifs are endlessly malleable and pertinent to present-day audiences who consume horror for its dissidence and provocation. Like the wider genre, body horror is constantly testing the boundaries of the acceptable and, in this act, re-imagining what cinema and fiction can do for us, the stories they can help us tell, the things we can dream of being and hopefully one day become.

2 Losing Control: Dehumanisation, Disease and Biotechnological Erasure

Loss of control is body horror's most determining narrative structure, broadly governing the advancement of plot and orchestrating many of its visceral spectacles.[22] Unruliness in this context has historically taken the shape of indecorous trespasses caused by moments in which biology temporarily fails or irrevocably overtakes protagonists. Accidental spillages, where not bombastic explosions, of abject, soiling fluids, catapult the realm of the private into the public eye, transgressing hard-learnt social lessons on the need for active restraint of physiological, involuntary acts. In metamorphic body horror, the moments where protagonists become partially or completely 'other(ed)' are punctuated by traumatic change or the growing or shedding of body parts, as well as the occasional development of 'forbidden', and sometimes deadly, appetites. It is no wonder that many body horror characters find themselves on the cusp of adolescence, a period ripe with 'growing pains' and the visible symptoms of puberty. Lack of bodily control can mediate concerns about regressing to childhood, a stage determined by desires and impulses that must be gradually trained into normative behaviours and their corresponding values. Yet that same rebelliousness can signal, and is often read as, an outburst of the bestial. As a reproductive process that imposes dramatic bodily change and involves parasitism of a sort, as well as potentially marks an entry into the adult role of parenthood, pregnancy is another transitional state favoured by body horror. Even in texts that celebrate the difference that emerges from transformation, such as *Ginger Snaps* (John Fawcett, 2000), acquired superpowers are first experienced with scepticism or panic. The new self runs the risk of

---

[22] In a short piece on the subgenre, director Stuart Gordon proposed that the 'best Body Horror makes your own body turn against you' (2012: 1). The self-harming element is key to the inescapability of its stock scenarios, or in his words: 'Your body is betraying you, and since it's your own body, you can't even run away' (1).

turning into a splenetic double in need of quashing for fear of the repercussions of its unleashing. Giving oneself over to deregulated drives has the significant drawback of turning us into threats to those who still live by the rules of the dominant social order. The lack of control in body horror combines scenarios where characters give in to provocative stimuli that prompt a rediscovery of the body with others in which external authority figures reify the *status quo* by force.

Contemporary body horror performs a careful dance between the aggressive anti-authoritarianism of extreme individualism and the hegemonic nature of society to denounce the ambiguity of the ideological systems that preside over the impartial materiality of life. The surveillance and normalisation associated with biopower, and which affect all social spheres, from the familial and educational to the medical and judicial, rely on defence, on security mechanisms that look after populations. Intrinsic to this regularisation is what Foucault calls a 'homeostasis' achieved by 'an overall equilibrium that protects the security of the whole from internal dangers' (2004: 249). In fact, subsequent biopolitical theories have used the 'immune system' (Haraway, 1989: 21–25) or 'immunity' (Esposito, 2013: 9–10) as metaphors for the methods that communities or collective bodies use to draw up boundaries and inoculate themselves. For Foucault, and Giorgio Agamben (1998: 4–10), death becomes justifiable via processes that 'separat[e] out the groups that exist within a population' (Foucault, 2004: 255), a subdivision of the species it controls via sets of prejudices like eugenics or the pathological discourse of medico-legal diagnosis. Studies have focused on the dehumanising necropolitics of empire (the enforced abduction, exploitation and murder epitomised by slavery) or states of exception, but biopower defines any form of violence against that which is perceived as 'inferior' or 'abnormal'. In the late twentieth and twenty-first centuries, biopower is increasingly carried out on the world stage, through the structuring of global territories imposed by transnational corporations, as Michael Hardt and Antonio Negri (2001: 31–4) argue, and the extraction of labour and resources from the Global South.

2.1 Less Than Human

The 'torture porn' cycle of the mid-noughties, if perhaps more interested in creating the memorable graphic set pieces after which it was named, nevertheless stands as a good rendition of the workings of necropolitics. The various mortifying contraptions in the *Saw* saga (2004–), centred around the corrective techniques of the Jigsaw killer and his disciples, offer a literal rendering of the punitive systems they ironically oppose. Jigsaw famously places his victims, alleged criminals, in escapable yet maiming traps intended to test one's desire to

live. The series borrows from religious beliefs, most notably Christian repent-
ance in the epiphanic outcomes it demands from its survivors, who will ideally
end up joining the murdering coterie, and the inscription of sin onto the body –
a 'lex talionis' that targets the human flaw and locates its corporeal simile. Since
victims have typically gone unpunished by a corrupt justice system, the
American myth of the vigilante is also invoked by the series. Jigsaw envisions
himself as a redeeming force, even though his self-righteous efforts are com-
promised by the fact that some subjects are unable to save themselves (their
lives rely on the actions of others), there is a big question mark over the
effectiveness of the 'tests' and, above all, the games often mistake the 'flawed'
individual for more abstract systems of inequality that transcend them. In Kevin
Greutert's *Saw VI* (2009) and *Saw X* (2023), members of a ruthless insurance
company and a scam clinic are punished for their fraudulent activities. Exactly
how guilty each person is remains vague, and larger problems, such as the
potential abuses of US health insurance businesses, remain untouched by this
neatly circumscribed excision of 'evil'. The *Saw* films are therefore best
understood as depressing explorations of the helplessness and dispossession
that have been in the zeitgeist following a major global crash and pandemic.
When taken as metaphors for larger biopolitical mechanisms, Jigsaw's traps
reveal how little faith we have of ever escaping the neoliberal games of
punishment that free-market deregulation has inflicted upon the financially
dispossessed, with their implication that the only aspect of human life that
matters is its use-value.

Eli Roth's *Hostel* (2005) was even more literal in its indictment of economic
hierarchies. The film follows a trio of American backpackers as they make their
way through a decadent Europe rife with iniquity and dishonesty and where
profit appears to drive every human interaction. In Slovakia, the sex-crazed
protagonists have the misfortune of falling into the clutches of Elite Hunting, a
members' club that assists rich clients in fulfilling their most macabre and
illegal fantasies, from rape to murder. There are some requisites: someone
must die as part of the transaction and, as the second film, *Hostel: Part II* (Eli
Roth, 2006), makes abundantly clear, no sentimental or contractual allegiances
will trump financial muscle if push comes to shove.[23] Elite Hunting grows from
a regional network preying on vulnerable tourists in the first instalment to
a multinational corporation by *Hostel: Part III* (Scott Spiegel, 2012), with
human goods defecting to the highest bidder within a closed community of
would-be torturers. To emphasise the commodification of the human body, and

---

[23] At the end of the film, the wealthy Beth (Lauren German) is able to buy her own freedom and the
death of her torturer by outbidding him.

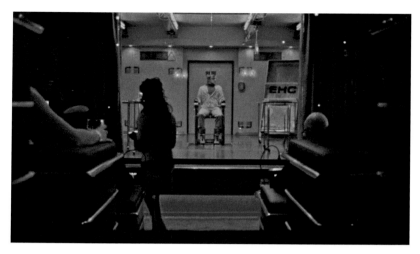

Figure 12 Torture and murder become entertainment for the wealthy.
Source: *Hostel: Part III*, directed by Scott Spiegel (Stage 6 Films, 2011)

therefore the dehumanisation of the victim-object, the setting of a new special facility is Las Vegas, a city self-billed as the 'Entertainment Capital of the World' and known for its gambling culture (Figure 12). *Hostel*'s repositioning of human bodies as purchasable items and 'experiences' may be ultimately dishonest in its victimisation of Westerners, yet there is a poignancy to the film's ability to metaphorise global structures of exploitation, such as forced labour and human trafficking. As an oppositional force, body horror confronts us with unpleasant truths, like how one's personal comfort and happiness comes at the expense of someone else's invisible suffering somewhere else in the world.

The contemporary internalisation of the monster, its relocation to the unreliable, torturous and haunting mindscapes of struggling protagonists, is both a telltale sign of the 'trauma turn' of twenty-first-century culture and the recognition that we are all involved in systems of oppression affecting others – if not on an individual level, then on a national or even species one. Concurrently, 'evil' is also now more readily associated with ethics. As in Mike Flanagan's reinterpretation of Edgar Allan Poe in the Netflix miniseries *The Fall of the House of Usher* (2023), where Gothic intergenerational strife calls out the abuses of Big Pharma through a thinly veiled critique of the Sackler family and the OxyContin crisis, villainy is most readily linked with characteristics like selfishness, greed, desire for power and lack of empathy. In contemporary horror, the monster is individuated through the figure of the corporation, itself embodied by a heartless boss and/ or its unscrupulous and despicable entourage. As in *Saw* and *Hostel*, these can be groups that enforce a particular set of necropolitical beliefs and practices or companies that work in the black market. Films such as *Anatomy* (Stefan Ruzowitzky, 2000) and *Turistas* (aka *Paradise Lost*, John Stockwell, 2006) revivify age-old surgical fears. In the former, a secret sect of anti-Hippocratic forensic doctors is discovered to be connected to experiments carried out in Nazi camps, and in the latter, a Brazilian ring responsible for 'live' organ harvesting is introduced as remorseless justice warriors who treat their (American) victims as a retributive resource through which the US can 'give back' some of what it has forcefully taken from their country. Inherent in this commercial enterprise is the primacy of violence and money, typically anathema to the ethical selfless donation substructure of transplantation.[24]

The workings of biopower find graphic echoes in other contemporary texts that exploit one of humanity's longest corporeal taboos: cannibalism. Anthropophagy in the popular imagination, as cautionary measure in folklore and legends, is multidimensional and feeds a number of monstrous fantasies about the release of 'the beast within' (Bourgault du Coudray, 2006: 5). Cannibalism's codification as transgressive act that depends on differentiation – on 'binary oppositions such as us vs. them, same vs. other, inside, vs. outside, good vs. bad' (Falk, 1994: 69) – is relevant to the work of biopolitics and necropolitics, not least because 'the slaughter and butchery that often precede it' are themselves seen as 'cultural . . . and moral abomination[s]' (Piatti-Farnell, 2017: 135). 'The human body is considered the pinnacle of the food chain' (Brown, 2013: 4), so cannibalism also threatens our artificial superiority and natural world pre-eminence by lowering the body to a consumer good (meat), even when it simultaneously infuses it with symbolism or ritualistic properties. In films like *We Are What We Are* (Jorge Michel Grau, 2010) and *Bones and All* (Luca Guadagnino, 2022), 'eaters' belong to outlaw communities who must keep themselves hidden from normative society and where victims are often chosen for their low status and perceived expendability.[25] A major trope of zombie and 'mondo' exploitation cinema in the 1970s and of serial killer fiction in the 1980 and 1990s, flesh-eating has continued to encapsulate social inequalities. Contemporary body horror is full of stories where the human body is stripped down to its base biology, where protective discursive and spiritual layers are removed by external forces and their sharp implements, where an entitled few resort to predatorial tactics and the helpless become fodder.

---

[24] Transplantation can also be prompted by financial necessity, rather than altruism. For more on the complex dynamics of transplantation and associated cultural histories, see Russell (2019) and Wasson (2020).

[25] At the end of *Bones and All*, Lee (Timothée Chalamet) is devoured whole by his lover, Maren (Taylor Russell), in what is prefigured as the ultimate act of love. This tenderness is not extended to all victims.

Figure 13 In cannibal horror, the elite typically feast on disenfranchised local 'produce'.

Source: *What You Wish For*, directed by Nicholas Tomnay (Evergreen Avenue, Jaguar bite and Freestyle Picture Company, 2023)

The frightful descent from social being to bare nourishment is allegorical because it never occurs in a cultural vacuum. For instance, the setting of *What You Wish For* (Nicholas Tomnay, 2023), a film about a wealthy elite with a taste for human specialties (Figure 13), is a very poignant Latin American rainforest and the 'produce' down-on-their-luck locals who, the hosts presume, will not be much missed by their communities. The film follows the actions of a conflicted gambler, Ryan (Nick Stahl), as he overcomes his initial reservations about killing people and reluctantly falls into the role of new specialist chef. This detail is important, as it highlights how moral integrity can be easily jeopardised by necessity or ambition. The fact that Ryan ends up being microchipped also evokes the panoptical core of financial exchanges: complicity in entering the world of commerce entails being subservient to one's employers and their enterprising vision. Texts like *What You Wish For* do not just elucidate the closed network of trade, of the need for demand to adapt to supply. They also reverse the colonial (and racist) assumption that cannibalism is a barbaric practice carried out primarily by exotic 'others'.[26] An appetite for human meat as an indicator of a discerning palate cannot be separated from access to exclusive delicacies, which are the prerogative of the 'corporate cannibal', the archetype of the high-end urbanite who is embedded in big business and obsessed by brands and competitive success – best epitomised by Patrick Bateman in Bret Easton Ellis's novel *American Psycho* (1991). The dog-eat-dog ethos and survival of the fittest logic

---

[26] See Kilgour (1998).

whereby the privileged 'buy' or prey upon the disadvantaged (often the destitute, sex workers or those who are unable to contribute their labour to society) is metaphorised in dystopias like Don LePan's *Animals* (2009), where the so-called 'mongrels' (humans born with disabilities caused by pollution) are deemed 'less than human', first by public perception and subsequently by the courts (2010: 57). The disenfranchised are also big game in fictions that descend from Richard Connell's short story 'The Most Dangerous Game' (1924). The gamification of murder in *Escape Room* (Adam Robitel, 2019), *The Hunt* (Craig Zobel, 2020) and the first season of the BBC series *Wreck* (2022–) is supported by the de facto maxim that some humans (the poorest) are less worthy than others. *The Purge* franchise (2013–2021), in which murder is decriminalised for twelve hours a year, already pointed to how such visions of social Darwinism build on existing systems of exclusion that disproportionately affect ethnic minorities and people in precarious financial positions. The popular series *Squid Game* (2021–), the most watched Netflix show ever on its year of release, joins a long chain of such representations that also includes the franchises *The Hunger Games* (2010–2020) and *Battle Royale* (1999–2005).

A gruesome strand of cannibal body horror transposes the torments typically visited upon the bodies of animals onto humans to remind us of an inconvenient reality: that 'the human' is a hierarchical construct that endows the human animal with a near-sanctity (as a reflection, or made in the image of, the divine) that is not granted to non-human animals.[27] Building on socially committed texts that sought to expose the cruelties and corruption of slaughterhouses – Upton Sinclair's novel *The Jungle* (1905), Georges Franju's documentary *Blood of the Beasts* (1949) or Archie Hind's novel *The Dear Green Place* (1966) – twenty-first-century novels like Joseph D'Lacey's *Meat* (2008) and Agustina Bazterrica's *Tender Is the Flesh* (2020 [2017]) envisage future societies where cataclysms have made humans the only meat available.[28] Both describe in painstaking detail meat processing, replacing animals with human specimens, to highlight the savagery involved in the modern industrialised handling of livestock. Unsurprisingly, the socially deprived – 'immigrants, the marginalised, the poor' (Bazterrica, 2020: 14) – fare much worse in such contexts. In *Tender Is the Flesh*, when Marcos, one of the workers, reflects on the epistemological violence required to turn people into a guilt-free product – 'us[ing] technical words to refer to what is a human but will never be a person' (16) – the novel invites us to apply the same logic to those groups less able to

---

[27] There are, of course, animal hierarchies too, with pets or 'sacred' animals receiving a very different treatment to those considered 'food'.

[28] Under the umbrella term 'the slaughterhouse novel', I discuss these texts at length in Aldana Reyes (2014: 97–121).

Figure 14 Humans replace cattle to decry the brutal cruelty of factory farming.
Source: *The Herd*, directed by Melanie Light (Eat Your Heart Out Films, 2014)

secure economic or legal protection. Women are also prized for their biological capacity to bear children. The jolting ending, in which a woman initially freed after seemingly gaining Marco's favour is pitilessly dispatched by him after she gives birth, is a final vicious echo of the misogyny that pervades the novel's dystopian world. *Meat* contains an additional layer of seditious critique aimed at the Church, whose religious stalwarts prove to be hypocritical and whose sanctification of human meat (victims are called 'the Chosen') functions less to grant solemnity than to justify thoroughly unchristian acts.[29]

These stories make it clear that the main impediments to stopping animal torture and slaughter are financial (business profits, dependent human livelihoods, national economies and resources) and epistemological (thinking of non-human animals as possessions and property, or the fact that 'personhood' is defined in opposition to animal consciousness in order to elevate the human). Hence, the focus is on shared characteristics between livestock and humans, like the ability to communicate, even without an intelligible language, to express sadness and pain, to bond and to form connections. Fantasies of people treated as cattle, which are not limited to cannibal fictions and include vegan activist texts like *The Herd* (Melanie Light, 2014), an award-winning short film that transposes the horrors of the dairy industry to women (Figure 14), are important because they raise issues about the law that have remained at the centre of discussions on biopolitics: who is kept inside or outside its frame and who becomes sacrificial victim to the system (Wolfe, 2013: 10). In other words, speciesism and the rights of animals, an important philosophical area that tests

---

[29] Shanti, a bolt-gunner, tells us that '[t]here was no soul in the meat, no spirit . . ., the sanctity of the flesh had died with its owners' (D'Lacey, 2008: 33). D'Lacey's novel thus critiques the biblical sanctioning of animal consumption.

Figure 15 Female meat is sold to rich men in *Fresh*.

Source: *Fresh*, directed by Mimi Cave (Hyperobject Industries and Legendary Pictures, 2022)

the limits of empathy and human selfishness, simultaneously reminds us of other political and social 'exclusions', of how human animals too can be marked out, for example in states of exception, by dint of race, religion, nationality or gender.

In *Fresh* (Mimi Cave, 2022), special cuts of human meat are labelled in plastic food bags with the victim's name and the date when they were 'produced' before being sent off by special mail delivery (Figure 15). The subscribers to Steve/Brendan's (Sebastian Stan) home business are shown to be decrepit, wealthy men who 'want the one thing that no one else has or can get' and the victuals exclusively female because 'that's where the market is'.[30] Cannibalism here is a mere motif that facilitates commentary on the real issue: the objectification of women. Opening with an example of blatant toxic masculinity (a man chiding his date for not projecting a traditionally female image), *Fresh* frames the relationship between heroine Noa (Daisy Edgar-Jones) and her torturer through the 'gaslight' tradition, evoking other 'woman as male object' narratives like the films *Poor Things* (Yorgos Lanthimos, 2023), *Captivity* (Roland Joffé, 2007), *Boxing Helena* (Jennifer Lynch, 1993) and John Fowles's novel *The Collector* (1963). Steve/Brendan is a chauvinist and domestic abuser – a scene implies he has eaten or sold one of his wife's legs – who gets a thrill out of overpowering women. In *Fresh*, cannibalism becomes another allegorical means through which to denounce how women are reduced to their bodies and the power play that still structures contemporary romance. It is telling that, as in other contemporary films directed or penned by women about abusive and misogynistic behaviours, such as *A Girl Walks Home Alone*

---

[30] The film also hints that they might belong to a Satanic cult.

at Night (Ana Lily Amirpour, 2014), *Revenge* (Coralie Fargeat, 2017) and *Promising Young Woman* (Emerald Fennell, 2020), Daisy saves herself with the help of other injured women, whom she first rescues.[31]

Jonathan Glazer's *Under the Skin* (2013) is a rare exception where cannibalism is aligned with the female world and the feminine body is weaponised to offer a powerful indictment of sexual harassment, which disproportionately affects women. Laura, played by an expressionless Scarlett Johansson, invites the attention of random men in the streets and nightclubs of Glasgow, a reversal of the pestering tactic, associated with rape culture, of men making unsolicited sexual advances on women in public spaces. Laura's pickups appear attracted to her vulnerability and gormless beauty, but in a surprise twist that sees the hunter become the hunted, the film reveals Laura to be a predacious creature in search of bodies to harvest. The 2000 Michel Faber novel of the same title provides more detail on the extraterrestrial origin of the protagonist, there named Isserley, and her mission to deliver human meat to her compatriots due to its scarcity in their home planet. The film substantially changes the ending, where readers are meant to empathise with Isserley's awakening to her own cog-in-the-machine expendability, to emphasise that its message is gendered. Just as Laura is growing more compassionate, she is molested by a forest logger who then tries to abuse her and eventually, when he discovers she is not human, burns her alive. Since the film forces an uncomfortable but nevertheless sustained alignment with Laura, her sudden and brutal death is not experienced as positive retribution against an invading alien species. It is hard not to read *Under the Skin*'s closing shot of the logger sententiously overlooking a mountain as anything other than a reminder that male violence is still a natural response to signs of female strength and difference.

New necropolitical horrors, from the 'live' removal of organs to on-demand butchers, hark back to the surgical nightmares of the mad science tradition. While Mary Shelley's *Frankenstein* has continued to inspire twenty-first-century artists, giving rise to meditations on the ethical implications of the creation of artificial intelligence like the film *Frankenstein* (Bernard Rose, 2015) and Jeanette Winterson's novel *Frankissstein: A Love Story* (2019), others have returned to the trope of the scientist/doctor as magician who can mould flesh and etch sinew into impossible and unspeakable new configurations. Characters like May (Angela Bettis) in *May* (Lucky McKee, 2002), Josef (Dieter Laser) in *The Human Centipede* (Tom Six, 2009) and Howard (Michael Parks) in *Tusk* (Kevin Smith, 2014) turn those unlucky enough to cross their

---

[31] Cassie (Carey Mulligan) dies in *Promising Young Woman*, but gets revenge on her abusers from beyond the grave.

paths into patchwork dolls, centipedes and walruses. Poesque fixations resulting from past trauma, marginalisation or unhealthy obsessions are normally the motivations for the outlandish transmogrifications. Like cannibalism, surgery is also a revenge tool. In *Hard Candy* (David Slade, 2005) and *American Mary* (Jen and Sylvia Soska, 2012), corrective scalpels are raised against offending males. In the former, a suspected sexual predator is made to believe he is being castrated alive; in the latter, a molester becomes a living canvas for bod-mod surgeon and survivor Mary (Katharine Isabelle). In rape-revenge texts, the gruesomeness of body horror can be curtailed by the bad behaviours of the 'victims', whose punishment is meted out in a savage fashion that mirrors the barbarity of sexual abuse. In *In My Skin* (Marina de Van, 2002), where Esther (played by the director and scriptwriter) performs acts of extreme self-harm like removing skin from her leg and preserving it, contemporary body horror has been able to merge feminist concerns over the sexist expectations imposed on women with the externalisation of psychological struggle. The film's subjective focalisation and ambiguous tone – scenes are sometimes shocking but also whimsical in Esther's rediscovery of herself – suggest the protagonist's assertion of agency and bodily autonomy in a world in which her looks and gestures have been carefully scrutinised by soulless and superficial business peers. As yet another strand of necropolitical body horror, surgical nightmares exhibit the body as mutable fabric and potential target of external attack, as exposed dermis vulnerable to extraneous inscription.

2.2 Diseased Bodies

The mad science tradition from which surgical horror descends finds another subsidiary in infection narratives, especially in stories where catastrophe is occasioned by unbridled technological progress or accidental laboratory leak-ages, as happens in *Contagion* (Steven Soderbergh, 2011) and Stephen King's novel *The Stand* (1978). Both of these texts were prescient in their fictional projections of origin stories for Covid-19 and the extent of global infrastructural collapse that a vicious-enough viral strain could cause. They also proved popular during the first lockdown (2020) with audiences, who turned to these narratives with a mixture of horror and speculative interest. Texts about pandemics are hardly a twenty-first-century phenomenon, but while the trope of the uncontrollable outbreak played an important role in late twentieth-century texts, contemporary body horror is preoccupied with what comes after, with the predicament of survivors. George A. Romero's post-millennial films were as prophetic in this sense as anything he directed in the twentieth century: *Land of the Dead* (2005), *Diary of the Dead* (2007) and *Survival of the Dead* (2009) all follow the implications of superspreader events, centring on the new forms of government and communication they propel. Given the limited length of films, it is perhaps inevitable that the most detailed investigations of zombie apocalypse survivalism would originate in comics and television, two mediums known for their seriality. *The Walking Dead* comic book series (2003–2019), created by Robert Kirkman and Tony Moore, and corresponding AMC series (2010–2022) resort to cyclical patterns, with protagonists in a constant process of re-establishing closed-off communities amid total chaos. These groups eventually lead to workable settlements and the re-imposition of earlier economic relationships, like bartering, that come under as much menace from internecine warfare as from zombie interference.

Our infatuation with the 'end times' is a clear reflection of a mounting awareness of the lasting impact and irreversibility of human action on our planet, a palpable disquiet also apparent in the gradual encroachment of the apocalypse, once a distinct but distant possibility and now a projection mere decades or years away from the text's publication or release date. The difficulties that characters experience in navigating future hostile environments in which resources are scarce and basic comforts have been replaced with stark endurance and the relative sturdiness of the latest barricade are already the present for nations suffering from unprecedented floods and droughts threatening to make whole nations disappear within a matter of years.[32] Now the fragility of ecosystems, animal extinctions, intergenerational equity and lack of viability of current systems of geopolitical power and distribution to weather the climate refugee crises are undeniable, the distance between reality and fiction has shortened, and an activist book like David Wallace-Wells's *The Uninhabitable Earth: A Story of the Future* (2019) becomes virtually indistinguishable in its cautionary rhetoric from the latest zombie dystopia. Infection horror texts tend to fetishise the family unit and the child as the embodiment of futurity, a motif that usually folds into that of the immune survivor and potential cure for humanity – for example, in the video game *The Last of Us* (2013) and the 2023 HBO series that adapts it – and the idea of 'community' rests on core values such as empathy, justice and collaboration. Reparation and damage control, as well as assertive ownership (of land, people, food), provide consolation and a sense of continuity and result in attempts to rebuild what was lost, as happens in Max Brooks's novel *World War Z: An Oral History of the Zombie War* (2006). Imbricated in such efforts of protection, reconstruction and (nationalistic) myth-building are elementary beliefs and assumptions about what

---

[32] These are disproportionately affecting developing countries like Nigeria, the Caribbean, West Asia and the Philippines (Law, 2019).

Figure 16 The pivotal moment when the human becomes 'other' is symbolic in zombie texts.

Source: 'Wildfire' (S1 E5), directed by Ernest Dickerson, *The Walking Dead* (AMC, 2010)

comprises the 'normal' and the 'other'. Indeed, one of the foremost quandaries taken up by contemporary zombie narratives is exactly what is worth preserving from the dying social order.

In inviting introspective examinations of what separates the self from the other, body horror demands biopolitical delimitations of the normative and its relation to exceptions. Infection horror construes this dichotomy through a binary: the 'healthy' body/person stands in opposition to the 'diseased' and infectious one. Shows like *The Walking Dead* place a particular emphasis on the thin line between the two states, for example, by having their characters look after loved ones until they tip over into the 'zombie' state, at which point they become dangerous and must be terminated (Figure 16).[33] Creating parallels between survivors and zombies, and portraying human villains as capable of a deliberate cruelty that far exceeds the mercilessness of the mindless horde, zombie texts sometimes collapse Manichean categories of good and evil to stress that what is deemed worth keeping alive is a matter of perspective and value judgement. This impulse to contest the notion of the 'diseased' as expendable bodies or subjects in need of containment is further prodded in texts where zombies, historically husks of their previous human selves driven by animal instinct and devoid of cognitive powers, gain sentience. The sympathetic zombie, popular in rom-zom-coms, serves as a make-believe substitute for real minorities who are discriminated against on the grounds of ethnicity,

---

[33] This is part of the plot of episode 5 of the first series, 'Wildfire', in which Andrea (Laurie Holden) keeps a wake for Amy (Emma Bell) until the very moment she comes back as a zombie, symbolically holding on to the last remnants of her sister's humanity.

sexuality or neurodiversity in texts like Daniel Waters's novel *Generation Dead* (2008), Bruce LaBruce's films *Otto; or, Up with Dead People* (2008) and *L. A. Zombie* (2010), S. G. Browne's novel *Breathers: A Zombie Lament* (2009) and Corey Redekop's novel *Husk* (2012). As with other contemporary horror texts, readers and viewers are asked to empathise with the ostensible 'monsters' and despise the real ones, who give away their moral evilness through acts of discrimination and abuse. Texts like Isaac Marion's *Warm Bodies* (2010) and The CW's series *iZombie* (2015–2019) go to the length of offsetting zombies' innate abjection by granting them superpowers such as the ability to relive other people's memories. In these narratives, the body horror of disintegration is a condition to keep under control, like chronic illnesses that require life-long medication, or else a 'flaw' that can be overlooked.

Infection horror is governed by an exponential proliferation that, unchecked, eventually overtopples whatever system life operated under before contagion reached epidemic proportions. Besides, zombies, in their guise as virological agents or brain-eating killers, are unappeasable, uncontainable and re-iterative, when not insidious.[34] Their insatiability and blind compulsion to devour without compunction or reason has made them the very distillation of consumer culture, as George A. Romero predicted in *Dawn of the Dead*, and a syndrome of free-market policies whose success comes at the cost of most individuals, developing countries and the environment.[35] A cipher for rampant post-industrial capitalism and its incompatibility with modern notions of sustainability, zombies are not just another version of 'us' but figureheads for a callous, apathetic 'marketplace' where respect for life is overridden by 'profit motive' (Webb and Byrnand, 2008: 91, 90). For Linnie Blake, zombie narratives allow audiences to work 'through the contemporary deliquescence of a body politic infected by neoliberalism' through their dismantling of that particular economic and ideological project and their call to wake up from the state of 'consumer-subject' ghoul into a politically engaged agency based around social reform (2015: 28). This point is driven home by corporatised biotechnologies that effectively operate as deregulated monopolies, as in the BBC series *In the Flesh* (2013–2014), where the zombie status can only be kept at bay through medication supplied by a governmental rehabilitation programme. Apart from exposing the political–legal enforcement of the contemporary medicalised subject, these supernatural scenarios fictionalise very real twenty-first-century predicaments like ongoing opioid crises, the abuses of the drugs industry in

---

[34] I am referring to texts like *The Walking Dead*, where infection has affected everyone, whether they have been bitten or not, and therefore all humans are zombies in waiting.
[35] See Quiggin (2010) and Giroux (2011).

holding on to specific patents for economic benefit or the Big Pharma scandals connected to Covid-19 vaccines.[36]

On the rise since emerging infectious diseases commanded attention in the 1970s and early 1980s due to outbreaks of genital herpes and HIV/AIDS (Ndow et al., 2019: 31), infection horror follows a pattern that the zombie apocalypse text incorporated and has even come to represent (Verran and Aldana Reyes, 2018). The release of the *Resident Evil* video games, the first of which appeared in 1996 and whose impact on the mutation of the zombie into shuffling biohazard is hard to overestimate, points to this change.[37] In infection horror, outbreaks throw countries, where not the entire world, into disarray before there is time to study the suspected pathogen or its origin. If enough characters progress into organised action, search parties are set forth with the mission to find scientific authorities and/or a cure, which can sometimes be synthesised out of immune carriers. These 'deus ex machina' characters are usually 'hybrids', as in M. R. Carey's *The Girl with All the Gifts* and the 2016 adaptation directed by Colm McCarthy, or Syfy's *Z Nation* series (2014–2018), where Murphy (Keith Allan), a 'blend', carries antibodies in his blood (Figure 17). The narrative goal and arc here are therefore

Figure 17 In *Z Nation*, the future is embodied by 'The Murphy', a genetic hybrid.

Source: 'The Murphy' (S2 E1), directed by John Hyams, *Z Nation* (Syfy, 2015)

---

[36] See Dearden (2023), Herzberg (2020) and Goldacre (2012).

[37] Before the late twentieth century, zombies were usually a product of black magic and, later, radiation or contamination. Classic examples include *White Zombie* (Victor Halperin, 1932), *Night of the Living Dead* and *Let Sleeping Corpses Lie* (Jorge Grau, 1974).

not significantly different from those of classical monster horrors. The collective aim is to understand, eradicate and/or domesticate the external threat so as to restore civic order. Infection narratives can in fact be thought of as a materialistic breed of previous forms of numinous fear. Whereas the Weird tradition of H. P. Lovecraft and Thomas Ligotti favours nihilistic fantasies in which humans find themselves belittled by cosmic forces that shatter their anthropocentric sense of mastery of the natural world, in infection horror the unknown world is more prosaic and microbiological in scope, if usually just as cynical.

Infection horror reduces the complexities of the self to a matter of physiology; it empties the human experience of anything other than virological processes of attack and defence. Races against time, such as the one at the heart of Paul Tremblay's *Survivor Song* (2020), a novel about a rabies-type outbreak in Massachusetts, leave little room for soulful exchanges or existential pondering. These are stories about the frailty of our immunological systems and where staying alive takes precedence. As Steven Shaviro argues, zombies enact an analogous species of materialist phenomenology because they 'are in a sense all body: they have brains but not minds . . ., they are nonholistic, deorganicized bodies: lumps of flesh that still experience the cravings of the flesh, but without the organic articulation and teleological focus' (1993: 86). This positivism is not necessarily a simplistic rendering of the human as animalistic or 'meat'. Instead, it vouches for a modern curiosity about the body, the internal mysteries and complaints that once remained the sole preserve of the medical profession but now animate programmes about bodily variance and exceptionalism like Channel 4's *Embarrassing Bodies* (2007–) and documentaries like the BBC's *Inside the Human Body* series (2011). Concomitant to this interest in biology is a growing awareness of mental health, well-being and self-care, which has led to a multi-billion fitness industry full of brands, magazines, personal trainers and twenty-four-hour gyms, themselves a late twentieth-century invention that has grown exponentially. The advent of image-centred social media, and especially its synergetic overlapping with product placement and advertising, has only intensified our corporeal fixation, bolstering the cosmetic and make-up industries. These phenomena indicate that the human body has been revalorised, no longer lowly and prosaic, but at the core of what we understand as essentially human – the key to our successes and pathologies, and even who and why we are.

Apart from betraying our biochemical present, where existential revelations do not stem from the discovery of Elder Gods or vengeful apparitions but of microscopic organisms and the 'invisible' lives of germs, infection horror shows the hallmarks of the disciplinary culture that determines body horror. In her foundational study of outbreak narratives, Priscilla Wald writes about how infection texts do not merely make microbes visible; they also 'chart . . . social interactions' to disclose 'an interactive and interconnected world', 'offer[ing] records of desire, of violence' (2008: 37–38). In a globalised context in which planes have made it possible for people to cross time zones and continents in a matter of hours, virological threats stand as the dark side of immediacy and the internationalisation of trade, as non-carbon footprints of human exchanges and activities. The linkages and dependencies made manifest by infection horror develop in their fictional counterparts into containment strategies, first organised by governments and, when these prove ineffective, martial law and guerrilla warfare. If democratic, liberal societies enact biopolitical regulations, the replacement of civilian governments with military powers, the worst epitome of which was the rise of fascist dictatorships in the first half of the twentieth century, stimulates a species of management of the living in relation to the infected or reanimated.

Since at least Romero's *Day of the Dead* (1985), zombie texts have been attuned to the underlying control structures of the modern state because they strip society of anything other than the surviving 'military-scientific complex, its chief mechanism for producing power and knowledge' (Shaviro, 1993: 94). Infection horror, and especially zombie pandemics and the metonymic equivalence between virus and the infected, offer textbook examples of the workings of necropolitics. Echoing the military outpost in *28 Days Later* (Danny Boyle, 2002) and Baghdad's Green Zone, District One in *28 Weeks Later* (Juan Carlos Fresnadillo, 2007) still stands as the most prominent case study of the exceptionalism of military rule. In this film, Britain is controlled by NATO following the outbreak of the Rage virus. A new area of 'safety and reconstruction' is set up in London's Isle of Dogs, but its Edenic veneer, epitomised by the appealing 'welcome back to Britain' slogan, soon cracks. The zone is under the control of the US army, who have unrestricted access to all buildings and administer the lives of 15,000 relocated civilians. Their presence is not just phantasmatic. In what amounts to a military version of Jeremy Bentham's panopticon, sniper rifle scopes and surveillance cameras scrutinise the lives of survivors (Figure 18), and freedom is sublated to careful supervision. That zombie texts are critical of these tracking apparatuses is evident not just from the way in which troops are depicted as frivolous and voyeuristic. Their efforts, like those of virtually every military group in zombie films, prove futile, at which point there is no dithering over annihilating the wider population. Body horror is naturally suspicious of disciplinarian strategies and of self-professed, populist leaders who wield power in the name of the masses. While endings in which viruses are never truly eradicated could be accused of a pessimism uncomfortably synonymous with detachment and apathy, and while there is a distinct failure in zombie texts to imagine a future

Figure 18 A sniper rifle sight doubles as camera lens in *28 Weeks Later*.
Source: *28 Weeks Later*, directed by Juan Carlos Fresnadillo (Fox Atomic and DNA Films, 2007)

that does not repeat the errors of the past, this type of body horror professes a unique distrust in the epistemological violence of biopolitical jurisdiction, of a future in which the 'diseased' body and the 'healthy' one are virtually indistinguishable, both subjected to the same methods of regulation and monitoring. Retrospectively, the national 'state of siege' decreed in *28 Weeks Later* turned out to be an uncanny analogue for the real global 2020–2021 Covid-19 lockdowns.[38]

2.3 Biotechnological Horror

Parasitism is a close cousin of infection horror and an equally old type of body horror. Essentially a form of predation in which an organism lives off and takes advantage from another, parasites have long been used creatively in Gothic and horror fiction, from nineteenth-century explorations of mesmerism in Arthur Conan Doyle's novella *The Parasite* (1894) and atavism in Bram Stoker's *Dracula* to twentieth-century tales of alien doubles such as John W. Campbell's novella *Who Goes There?* (1938) and Jack Finney's Cold War allegory *The Invasion of the Body Snatchers* (1955). In the 1980s, the technohorror of *The Fly* and *Tetsuo*, particularly the films' grotesque hybrid protagonists (part-human, part-insect or machine), signalled the evolution of the trope in a new context defined by the dogmatic predominance of science and where technology (analogue in the first

---

[38] The term is Paul Virilio's, but my usage here is indebted to the deployment in Botting (2010: 161).

instance, then digital and virtual) had begun not just to inflect the shape of the human (the transhumanism of bionic bodies) but to radically reframe subjectivity. Cronenberg's hallucinogenic melding of person and recreational machine to the point of ontological indistinction – the videotape player–man in *Videodrome* and the bio-ported player in e*Xistenz* (1999) – resonated with the Baudrillardian ethos of simulacral films like *The Lawnmower Man* (Brett Leonard, 1992) and *The Matrix* (The Wachowskis, 1999). Much as William Gibson had already cautioned in his visionary *Neuromancer* (1984), the escapist fetish for virtual otherworlds has to contend with the physicality of the flesh, for even when the mind is free to travel, it remains anchored to the visceral materiality of the body. The integrity of embodiment has been put into question by transhumanists like Hans Moravec and Ray Kurzweil, who believe in the eventual and inevitable transference of human consciousness, in their view a computable process, onto electronic devices and networks. If even promises of a smaller scale connected Metaverse have yet to materialise at the time of writing, it is perhaps a truism that, in the twenty-first century, Western subjectivity is not merely refracted but constructed from online projections like digital avatars, social media profiles, 'live' community gaming and image filters.

In light of body horror's technological determinism, sceptics may reasonably interrogate the boundaries of body horror vis-à-vis science fiction. Both speculative in their visions of the future and present, science fiction tends to err on the side of speculative optimism, while horror is, by virtue of its trappings, geared towards pessimistic outlooks on technological advancement or on their repercussions for older framings of the human. Texts about AI and cloud consciousness like *Her* (Spike Jonze, 2013) and *Lucy* (Luc Besson, 2014) are not horrific, even when they do not shy away from the potential negative impacts of the innovations that energise their narratives. Darker texts, like *Ex Machina* (Alex Garland, 2014), though clear descendants of the Frankenstein tradition, could be labelled scientific thrillers by some.[39] There can be little doubt, however, when considering the generic ascription of tense, dispiriting and grisly films like *Event Horizon* (Paul W. S. Anderson, 1997) and *Life* (Daniel Espinosa, 2017) and video games like the *Dead Space* series (2008–). Body horror of this kind is logically inflected by science fiction through its setting, characters and themes, yet it remains fundamentally suspicious about the place of the human in tomorrow's technocracies, not least because these are seen as offshoots of big necropolitical corporations that continue the work of colonialism. Ridley Scott's pioneering film *Alien* already featured characters subservient to

---

[39] Some critics see all cyborg texts as 'Mary Shelley's stepchildren' (Friedman and Kavey, 2016: 146, 185–90).

'technological totalization, where every part of life is alienated and infiltrated by institutions and agents operating within the global machine of capitalism' (Webb and Byrnand, 2008: 93) and where the crew is ultimately expendable. The extractivist motivation behind 2020s missions to Mars, a planet containing precious materials to be mined economically, spells out the worry that the Earth will soon run out of certain natural resources.

At heart, new body horror is preoccupied with the consequences of the biotechnological revolution on the human. Progress in this area chiefly centres on genetic engineering, mostly used in the synthesising of medical substances and the manipulation of DNA sequencing in animals and plants to maximise production and increase resistance to pesticides (GMO foods). What has captured the creative imagination, though, are the applications that seek to transform human biology. Stem cell research and nanotechnology, currently used in the engineering of tissue and therapeutic cancer treatments, as well as cloning, have given rise to all manners of biochemical horrors, including the films *Body Melt* (Philip Brophy, 1993), *Isolation* (Billy O'Brien, 2005), *Repo Men* (Miguel Sapochnik, 2010), *Upgrade* (Leigh Whannell, 2018) and the *Resident Evil* franchise (2002–2021), Michael Crichton's novel *Prey* (2002) and the *Bioshock* video-game series (2007–2016). The porosity between genres is once again manifest here, for mainstream science-fiction films like *Gattaca* (Andrew Niccol, 1997), the *Jurassic Park* franchise (1990–) and *Never Let Me Go* (Mark Romanek, 2010) have also prodded the moral grey areas of genetic engineering. The Darwinian fears that fuelled *Alien*, specifically the Xenomorph's perfect adaptation to its environment, predatorial precision and parasitic use of the human body as incubator, resurface in films like the *Species* series (1995–2007).[40] This franchise also capitalises on the categorical indistinctions that populated body horrors of the 1980s like *The Thing* and *The Fly*, creating their nightmarish visions by fusing together 'elements . . . that offend the moral or natural order of things' (Luckhurst, 2021: 229). The Weird tradition, at least in its Lovecraftian slant, concocts unnameable horrors that test the limitations of the human mind to process creatures so inherently incompatible with our natural world that they 'can not [*sic*] be described' (Lovecraft, 1928: 177), only approximated via comparison to known genera. Categorical indeterminism treads most decisively on body horror grounds when bizarre forms bear at least some resemblance to the human. In a direct line from Mary Shelley, but especially H. G. Wells's 'Beast Folk' in *The Island of Doctor Moreau* (1896), post-millennial texts turn to genetic splicing as a biotechnological equivalent of older vivisectionist scalpels and alchemical

---

[40] This link is strengthened by the fact that Swiss artist H. R. Giger designed the extraterrestrials for both franchises.

transmutations. Dren (Delphine Chanéac), in *Splice* (Vincenzo Natali, 2009), a human–animal hybrid whose unique DNA make-up remains ambiguous, is feared because her body develops quicker than expected and, as her gender switch attests, she is generally unpredictable. Notwithstanding her murderous tendencies, Dren also enters the uncanny valley of the 'abhuman' because her existence endangers species purity and the implied supremacy of her makers. Through her, '[t]he human body ... reveals its morphic computability with, and thus lack of distinction from, the whole world of animal life including those species occupying different lines of descent' (Hurley, 1996: 103). As it did for fin-de-siècle texts, the absence of individualising factors raises the spectre of atavism and disrupts conventional animal hierarchies. Ridley Scott's *Prometheus* (2012) and *Alien: Covenant* (2017) even reverse the classical Promethean myth by making humans the biochemical product of a superior alien race (Figure 19).

Appreciation for the fraught and composite relationships between humans and nature has been instrumental in promoting environmental activism like the Extinction Rebellion movement, founded in 2018. The same impetus is responsible for the blossoming of what has come to be known as 'new materialism(s)', or a millennial theoretical turn 'seek[ing] to critique anthropocentrism's presumption of matter as inherently passive and devoid of meaning' (Gamble et al., 2019: 112) and which understands reality not through individuation but the interconnectivity of 'intra-actions' between 'entangled material agencies' (Barad, 2007: ix, 66). Out of this intellectual backdrop emerged notions of the transcorporeality of the human that challenge its separate agency and instead present the body as 'substantially and perpetually interconnected with the flows of substances and the agency of environments' (Alaimo, 2012: 476). Body horror has kept its visceral finger firmly on this ecological and new materialist pulse by, for example, conjuring up nightmares of

Figure 19 In *Prometheus*, humanity is the result of recombined part-alien DNA.
Source: *Prometheus*, directed by Ridley Scott (Twentieth Century Fox, 2012)

fungus–human symbiosis or hybridisation, such as Silvia Moreno-Garcia's novel *Mexican Gothic* (2020), the film *Gaia* (Jaco Bouwer, 2021) and T. Kingfisher's novella *What Moves the Dead* (2022). In the visually mesmerising *Color Out of Space* (Richard Stanley, 2019), humans and animals (alpacas) fuse to create new and strange combinations that fly in the face of conventional genetics. In David Cronenberg's *Crimes of the Future*, a radical cell of 'evolutionists' modify their digestive systems to be able to consume the abundant human-produced plastic and toxic waste littering the world (Figure 20). And in the case of the experimental film *Upstream Color* (Shane Carruth, 2013), entanglement is turned into a literal metaphor through a plot based on the linked psychological interdependence between animals (humans, larvae, pigs) and flora (orchids). The bewildering amalgamated bodies of body horror move past conventional concerns about species uniqueness because they are inter-polated by guilt and a determined desire to shake off the type of anthropocen-trism that has led to natural devastation on an unprecedented scale. Behind reactionary adaptive fears hides a more positive take on genetic splicing fascinated by the plasticity and transgenic affiliation between all forms of life. In 'our age of time-lapse photography, electron microscopy, and pene-trating documentaries' (Asma, 2009: 198), the human becomes ever further atomised and reconceived as an intricate microbiome.

The biotechnological laboratories and clinics of body horror undergo a serious scrutiny that seeks to question the ethics and procedures of certain

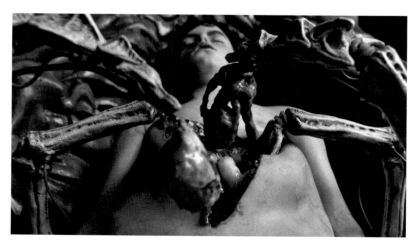

Figure 20 Public autopsies help map the chaos of accelerated evolution in *Crimes of the Future*.

Source: *Crimes of the Future*, directed by David Cronenberg (Serendipity Point Films, Téléfilm Canada and Ingenuous Media, 2022)

medical sectors. Surgical cosmetic procedures have regularly made headlines in the early 2020s due to botched procedures and deadly operations taking place in countries like Turkey. In the *Rabid* remake (The Soska Sisters, 2019), after a disfiguring car accident, Rose (Laura Vandervoort) undergoes a pioneering stem-cell treatment that restores her beauty but has unexpected side effects. The fashionista's new-found voraciousness does not just typify the greed of an industry where money can matter more than the safety of patients, but also exposes the cruelties of the fashion industry, much as Nicolas Winding Refn did with *The Neon Demon* (2016). In Brandon Cronenberg's even more coruscating *Antiviral* (2012), the cult of personality and body fetishism lead to a new genetic market for viruses, attractive because they give the illusion of intimacy and closeness, and to Astral Bodies, a company that sells meat grown from the cells of celebrities. In *Infinity Pool* (Brandon Cronenberg, 2023), the entertainment industry and the judiciary intersect. For an extortionate fee, tourists convicted of crimes are allowed to have the police execute a clone in their stead. Although these victim-perpetrators are not born and raised, rather fabricated in a medical environment, the film is interested in the ethics of innocence and identity transference. Its denouement asks whether, in the process of witnessing his own execution countless times, James (Alexander Skarsgård) has not risked his sense of ontological certainty.

Texts like *Rabid*, *Antiviral* and *Infinity Pool* are perhaps best defined by the term 'biopunk', a subgenre interested in biotechnology's often unintended, detrimental effects. Coined by Brian McHale, biopunk (rendered 'bio-punk' in the original) is understood as a biological cyberpunk sub-variety that 'revise[s], update[s] and rationalize[s] classic Gothic-horror motifs of bodily invasion and disruption' (1992: 257) and is less preoccupied with the creation of robotic life than with the growing or cloning of individuals or the bio-technical extension and augmentation of physical and psychological abilities. Although many of the texts designated as biopunk sit more comfortably within the parameters of science fiction, since the threat of 'bodily fusion' and 'physical diffusion' (257) are one of its concerns, some texts have bordered on body horror. For example, in the 2022 video game *Scorn*, combat is enabled once the humanoid protagonist is attacked by a creature that attaches itself to his body and slowly begins to take over. Biomechanical weapons made of strange configurations of what look like alien flesh and reptilian metal connect to the living tail of the creature. By the end of the game, host and parasite merge into a tortured organic totem that, like the rest of the game, recalls the dark art of H. R. Giger and Zdzisław Beksiński, the visual inspiration for the design and settings (Figure 21).

Body horror's technophobia is not constrained to futuristic extraterrestrial landscapes. In the wake of Marshall McLuhan's influential understanding of

Figure 21 Biopunk is shaped by the aesthetic history of body horror.
Source: *Scorn*, developed by Ebb Software (Kepler Interactive, 2022)

technology as an 'extension of consciousness' (2001: 4), contemporary body horror has turned its attention to techno-subservience. Films like *Sequence Break* (Graham Skipper, 2017) and *Peripheral* (Paul Hyett, 2018), in which person and programme (an arcade video game in the former, AI software in the latter) mutate into hallucinogenic and claustrophobic admixtures of flesh and electronic data, seem to make the point that our relationship with technology is one of dependence to the point of indivisibility. As machines and the internet have gained the ability to articulate and even predict human behaviours through, for example, biometrics and 'data exhaust' (Zuboff, 2019: 68), creator and creation become harder to pick apart. At the heart of such body horrors lie ages-old anxieties about technology, notably that one of its likely side effects is alienation and isolation and that machinic emancipation may lead to a loss of control, a presumption that has powered both fiction (robotic dystopias) and actual reporting on the AI revolution.[41] Even in texts that depict the alliance between person and technology as predominantly productive, some reservation is detectable. Julia Ducournau's indefinable *Titane* (2021), about Alexia (Agathe Rousselle), a dancer with a titanium plate who appears to become pregnant after having sex with a car, is a good case in point. While the film's final image is hopeful – Vincent (Vincent Lindon), traumatised by the disappearance of his biological son, embraces a newborn with a titanium spine, and whispers 'I'm here' (Figure 22) – the mother dies during labour. *Titane*

---

[41] As a small but pertinent sample, see Cuthbertson (2023) and Vallance (2023).

Figure 22 Old models of the human are left behind in the ambiguous conclusion to *Titane*.

Source: *Titane*, directed by Julia Ducournau (Kazak Productions and Frakas Productions, 2021)

presents new human–machine assemblages born out of our technological fetish and hints at a symbiotic future that upgrades, but possibly also erases and fundamentally rethinks, the human.

There is a deeper sense in which biotechnological horror acts as a mouthpiece for contemporary concerns. In his assessment of the peculiarities of the horror genre from the 1990s onwards, Jason Colavito diagnoses a tangible 'helplessness' and 'fatalism' in popular texts emerging from post-millennial 'scientific conceptions about the mind' (2008: 349). For him, the reigning scientific materialism, in particular the demystification of consciousness brought about by the advent of MRI scans and experiments involving the electrical stimulation of the brain, put a stop to earlier fables about free will, the existence of the soul and the supposed mastery of our bodies. He singles out a representative article by Steven Pinker, published in *Time* magazine in 2007, where the renowned cognitive psychologist explained that science had proven without a doubt that 'every aspect of consciousness can be tied to the brain' (Pinker, 2007: 62), including notions of selfhood. For many, this meant that humans were now best conceived as 'nothing but meat machines playing out preprogrammed roles' (Colavito, 2008: 355), a new form of technobiopolitics. Dripping with existential angst, contemporary body horror constitutes a mourning for the present – not just for a prelapsarian notion of pure, organic, pre-digital, non-augmented subjectivity, but for a past where we could think of ourselves as holistic, irreplaceable beings. Biotechnological horrors ultimately rest on loss of control, in this case to our own high-tech offspring and the prejudices and value judgements they replicate. External systems of oppression that dehumanise its victims are replaced in these fictions with the de-anchoring of modern industrial citizens, bewildered by a chaos of automated services and unfettered AI, dreading their redundancy and duplication.

3 Embodied Identity: Feminist, Queer and Black Body Horror

This book has thus far largely concerned itself with necropolitical operations that reduce the human to biology, stripping people of rights and social meaning through forms of epistemic violence that can be both personal (individual) or collective (corporate, political, legal). The self becomes 'othered', objectified and subdued into a lesser, agentless state without protective safeguards. Bodies and the personalities they contain are always at risk of losing their assumed independence, imperilled by behaviours, structures, practices or technologies that can take freedoms away and replace them with brutal states of subjugation. Insofar as it is preoccupied with our biological 'otherness', body horror's interest lies in our capacity to be altered by extrinsic forces and the impact that this fact has on our conceptions and presumptions about ourselves – our free will, privileges and perception of singularity. Understandably, necropolitical ordeals leave little room for cheerful reclamations of the positive powers of change.

Yet there is another significant strand of body horror, on a steady rise since the mid-2010s, that counterbalances the power structures denounced by body horror with the potentialities bestowed by metamorphosis. This politically minded horror is frequently authored by members of communities that have experienced discrimination because of one or several aspects of their identity. The horrific elements in their work still speak to oppression and the fear inherent in the process of corporeal transformation is in synch with basic worries about the loss of a stable sense of the self, but metamorphic horrors find joy and value in challenging the norm. In designing new corporeal realities for their protagonists, or what may be termed new 'corpo-realities', body horror suggests that alternatives to existing models of subjectivity and sociopolitical inequalities are possible. Despite the fact that protagonists may not always be granted a happy ending, body horror's narratives can promote the need for diversity and emphasise flux, or the idea that bodies are sites in process. The transgressive disruption that the self–other in these texts supposes typically denounces the constructed nature of stigmatisation, systemic inequality and social exclusion. In fact, this new body horror often mobilises pro-feminist, sexually unprejudiced, trans-inclusive and anti-racist messages, and makes a strong case for social change. Its overall optimism may incline some to use terms like 'magic realism' or 'dark fantasy', but reading this cultural development as a new phase in the history of body horror allows us to extend the subgenre's reach and substantiates the argument that its concerns are politically engaged, timely and ideologically valuable. In this respect, body horror is in line with the ethical spirit of the Gothic mode, which has recalibrated sympathy for the monstrous and sweetened macabre imagery to make it palatable to younger audiences, especially in the twenty-first century.

Body horror fleshes out 'otherness' because the 'normal' body is exposed as a normative fiction. The day-to-day discussion, representation and management of bodies construct a series of '"truths" and norms' that demand 'an opposing field of the *un*natural and deviant' (Atkinson, 2005: 4, italics in the original). Given that the interplay of the physical/biological and the social/cultural is so stark as to have 'underpinned the development of the kinds of disciplinary specialization that have led to a split between the natural and human sciences' (Blackman, 2008: 3), body horror could be accused of joining together a number of distinct processes of corporeal exclusion and inequality, many of which overlap. I acknowledge this limitation and narrow the scope to encompass gender, sexuality and ethnicity, embodied characteristics explored assiduously by the subgenre. Such traits are not taken as discrete entities, even though one of the virtues of body horror is that, in segregating biases, it renders them conspicuous and discernible. This section takes as its starting point the principle that metamorphic body horror partakes of, and relies on, comparable acts of prejudice, bigotry and biological essentialisms, or what Richard Dyer describes as a 'felt connection' (1997: 6) between social differences and stigmas.

3.1 Feminist Body Horror

Groups that have historically been discriminated against have gravitated towards body horror because it is able to expose biopolitical biases through its representational strategies. Women, queer people and ethnic minorities are the focus here, but other types of bodies are regularly reduced to their biology by medical and social practices that 'other' and even caricature them.[42] While some inroads have been made, biological essentialisms are particularly pronounced and still constantly applied to women. Their bodies are more socially policed than men's and routinely dissected for 'flaws' by the media and tabloids: bodies are too thin, too big, too sagging, too artificial, too desperate to look youthful. Since the coining of 'metrosexuality' in the 1990s and the blossoming of the male beauty industry, which has led to *Men's Health* becoming the bestselling magazine for men in the UK and the US, male bodies are progressively being placed under a similar microscope. Yet the level of scrutiny pales by comparison. It is telling that plastic surgery and the use of injectables like Botox and filler are at an all-time high, with

---

[42] Body Studies typically also investigates disablism, fat shaming, ageism and classism, among other expressions of bodily stigmas imposed on specific groups.

new patients getting ever younger (Heron-Langton, 2019; Kato, 2023). Beauty is still a monetisable source of professional success for women, nowhere more so than in social media, home to endless make-up tutorials and cosmetic tips that themselves put further pressure on the need to always look one's best.[43] Sexism is not skin deep, though. As Niall Richardson and Adam Locks argue, '[w]hile men have always been associated with reason, intellect and scholarship (the "great" minds of civilization have always been *assumed* to be men) . . ., women are enthralled to nature', conflated with their bodies in their association 'with all bodily activities like pregnancy, birth and breast feeding' (2014: 8–9, italics in original). Women living in places where abortion is not legal are all too aware that these conceptual subtractions, founded on taboos and social and religious norms, have practical disciplinary correlatives. Between menstruation and menopause, control over women's bodies is, to a greater or lesser extent, made available to other people and official institutions (DeMello, 2014: 59). And as Women Studies have taught us, after this period, those same bodies then fall into the category of the 'female grotesque' (Russo, 1995: 62–63), an archetype that inspires laughter and derision.

Horror has responded to this state of play with the figure of the 'monstrous-feminine', an ambiguous prototype of abjection that both captures sexist attitudes and, in Barbara Creed's theorisation, represents a disruption of the patriarchal symbolic order (1993: 6–7). Its exaggeration of women's reproductive functions takes the shape of the ghastly, overprotective mother, 'an antagonist who provokes negative masochistic fantasies of death, engulfment, and/or eradication' (Arnold, 2013: 33), as well as its budding opposite, the dangerous young girl on the cusp of adolescence whose unruly body and dark cravings cannot be repressed. Novels such as Neil Gaiman's novel *Coraline* (2002) and Ainslie Hogarth's *Motherthing* (2022) and the films *The Others* (Alejandro Amenábar, 2001), *Mama* (Andrés Muschietti, 2013), *The Babadook, Goodnight Mommy* (Matt Sobel, 2014), *Hereditary, Evil Dead Rise* (Lee Cronin, 2023) and *Beau Is Afraid* (Ari Aster, 2023) are proof that the twenty-first century has seen no shortage of 'monstrous' mothers. Contemporary texts have also returned to another archetype, one initially popularised by *Rosemary's Baby* (Roman Polanski, 1968): the beleaguered and helpless pregnant woman whose baby is under threat of extraction for nefarious purposes by outsiders. *Inside* (Julien Maury and Alexandre Bustillo, 2007), *The Womb* (Fajar Nugros, 2022), *Huesera: The Bone Woman* (Michelle Garza Cervera, 2023) and FX's streaming series *American Horror Story: Delicate* (2023–2024) turn the tables by making mothers-to-be the victims of interference and exploitation. Implicit in these texts,

---

[43] See Berkowitz (2017).

Figure 23 Feminist body horror mediates the psychosomatic complexities
of pregnancy.

Source: *Huesera: The Bone Woman*, directed by Michelle Garza Cervera (Disruptiva
Films, Machete Producciones and Maligno Gorehouse, 2023)

but explicit in others, is a biological fear over the changes that women's bodies
undergo when expecting and during the postpartum period (Figure 23). Films
such as *Honeymoon* (Leigh Janiak, 2014), *Devil's Due* (Matt Bettinelli-Olpin and
Tyler Gillet, 2014), *Prevenge* (Alice Lowe, 2016), *Antibirth* (Danny Perez, 2016)
and *Bed Rest* (Lori Evans Taylor, 2022) utilise body horror not just to convey
natural fears about hormonal and physical changes, the uncanny feeling of
having life growing inside one's body and the tragic possibility of significant
complications or miscarriage. As Erin Harrington proposes, in pregnant horror
'woman's subject-position tends to become subordinate to that of the foetus'
(2016: 97). The ensuing conflict, where 'the borders and capacities of the body are
actively contested, erased and sometimes redrawn' (97), is of necessity an enquiry
into the limits of selfhood and otherness. Motherhood changes a woman's social
position and perception, and as horror declaims, this is accompanied by
a cloistering of the body within domestic spaces and its corseting within
a series of expectations, both moral (bringing up children) and aesthetic (recuperating one's physical shape after the real body horror of parturition). By switching
roles and making young males, rather than the female nurses who look after them,
bear the embryos of the future with great risk to their own lives, a film like the
enigmatic *Evolution* (Lucile Hadžihalilović, 2015) draws attention to this sacrificial underside of reproduction.

The motherhood trope is not confined in its creative powers to the reproduction of systems of oppression and states of existential confusion. In some

instances, abjection can be appropriated in a carnivalesque fashion too. Taking her cue from Angela Carter's bestial women in the collection *The Bloody Chamber* (1979), Rachel Yoder's *Nightbitch* introduces readers to an initially agreeable, subservient mother who suddenly becomes a savage and voracious nocturnal animal, the 'Nightbitch' of the title. Living in a middle-class world of posturing that rewards ideals of perfect motherhood, the protagonist struggles to hold her life together under the pressure of external expectations on the way she should look, act and think after having her child. Growing fur and a tail become an analogy for the biological changes experienced during and after the liminal state that is pregnancy, but Nightbitch is also a Mrs Hyde, a mythical doglike figure that offers freedom and the shameless fulfilment of forbidden desires because '[s]he can be a body and instinct and urge. She can be hunger and rage, thirst and fear, nothing more. She can revert to a pure, throbbing state' (Yoder, 2022: 83). Raw animal corporeality, summoned by anger and hopelessness, disturbs gendered norms and social mores, and makes up for feelings of frustration and stasis. As I have been arguing about body horror more widely, Yodel's novel is aware that this repressed 'other' is really a part of the self. The narrator tells us that '[s]he wanted to think she had become another person altogether the night before, but she knew the horrible truth, that Nightbitch had always been there, not even that far below the surface' (9). The reinforcement of her true nature comes hand in hand with an unapologetic embrace of her creative powers as both artist and giver of life. Body horror thus becomes a conductive medium for positive behavioural and psychological progress.

Nightbitch is a doglike monster belonging to the female werewolf tradition. As Hannah Priest argues, werewolves' associations with 'hunting, savagery and aggression' (2015: 3) have typically gendered them as male, and while their female counterparts draw on shared cultural assumptions and ideas (the release of the beast within), there are also recurring tropes that predominate in she-wolf fictions: social exclusion as shared experience, entrapment within patriarchal structures (and the wish to break out from them), the bestial state as threat to domesticity and the feminised (hyper)sexualisation of the shapeshifter (10–16). All of these can be observed in a text that has become the contemporary standard for this subgenre: *Ginger Snaps*. In the film, the onset of adulthood, Ginger's (Katharine Isabelle) first period, coincides with an attack that gradually transforms her into a dangerous werewolf. The film's mapping of the indignities of teenage bodies, their unexpected changes, onto lycanthropic metamorphosis are primarily grounded in female experiences of adolescence and the high levels of scrutiny teenage girls are under. Ginger's bestial turn coincides with her sexual awakening and stylisation into a *femme fatale* who bites back (Figure 24) and takes the dominant role in her relationship with 'bad boy' Jason (Jesse

Figure 24 The she-wolf transformation marks a confidence-boosting entry into sexual maturity in *Ginger Snaps*.

Source: *Ginger Snaps*, directed by John Fawcett (Oddbod Productions, 2000)

Moss) and then makes advances on Sam (Kris Lemche). Ginger, much like the possessed Jennifer (Megan Fox) in Karyn Kusama's *Jennifer's Body* (2009), is a whirlwind of barely controlled emotion and retributive power shaking the foundations of suffocating models of femininity that have insisted in tweens remaining passive, quiescent, shy, cute and straitlaced. Ginger's revolt is ultimately sabotaged by her loving sister, Brigitte (Emily Perkis), in a tragic denouement that, as Sue Short points out (2006: 106–09), questions the character's potential as alternative antihegemonic mode of identification, but simultaneously highlights the importance of female kinship to the werewolf narrative and to female-led body horror. Feminist texts propose sisterhood as one way to tackle sexism.

Both *Ginger Snaps* and *Nightbitch* undertake similar conceptual work to that explored by the related 'feral woman' narrative. In such texts, the protagonist does not transform into a physical beast but a trigger sparks off a wild psychological and behavioural state. Like the werewolf, and indeed the ungovernable double, the new self flies in the face of social and gendered propriety and causes havoc if not carefully monitored. In Julia Ducournau's *Raw* (2016), Justine's (Garance Marillier) ontological passage is marked by the forced ingestion of a rabbit kidney, particularly symbolic given she happens to be a vegetarian veterinary medical student. The transition is borne out by a skin rash, a sign that the change has affected Justine somatically (Figure 25). She soon finds herself having strong cravings for meat that quickly escalate into devouring a human

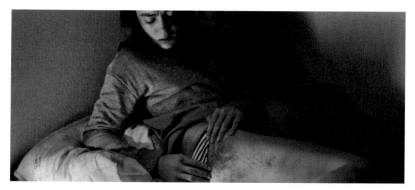

Figure 25 A nasty skin rash marks the start of Justine's meat cravings in *Raw*.
Source: *Raw*, directed by Julia Ducournau (Petit Film, Rouge International and Frakas Productions, 2016)

finger. These acts are set against the uninhibited background of a week-long series of hazing rituals full of drugs, sex and degrading activities. *Raw* thus presents the start of higher education as yet another barbaric process of initiation mirroring the onset of adulthood and full of new dangers to one's sense of self and integrity, foremost of which is the pressure of social assimilation. Noticeably, *Raw* is a lot more optimistic in its conclusion than earlier feminist body horror films, for there is no punishment meted out to the heroine. When Justine finds out her hunger runs in the family, her father, shown to be complicit to the level of having his own lip and chest mauled by his wife, proclaims she will find a solution.

The feral self is catapulted by social repression and stands as its direct embodiment. It is therefore simultaneously a negative metaphor and a sublimation of its catalysts. In Aronofsky's *Black Swan*, lonely ballet dancer Nina (Natalie Portman) finds herself caught in cycles of microaggression perpetrated by her overprotective mother, a rapacious artistic director and a cast of resentful dancers. Her figurative transformation into the Black Swan at the end of Pyotr Ilyich Tchaikovsky's *Swan Lake* (1875–1876) is prefaced by a long list of transgressions that separate mature Nina from her childish, mollycoddled past. Drinking, sex and drugs all act as disinhibitory elements that loosen up her feral self, the dark swan of sensuality and success. Since, in the film, this figure is also connected to the destructive pitfalls of professional fixation, and given ballet's reinforcement of pronounced gendered roles, Nina's death at the end can be read as both the annihilation of her innocent, guarded and infantilised self and an indictment of the inordinate expectations placed on the bodies of female athletes. The body horror in *Black Swan* is somatic too, with scenes of Nina's demanding training routinely climaxing in moments of acute pain (ankles cracking and succumbing to body weight, nails splitting). These occurrences should not be entertained as sadistic voyeurism, but as productive critiques of biopower that seek to make oppression intelligible and intimately close. As Steen Leder Christiansen argues, texts like *Black Swan* encourage audiences to 'feel *with*', 'not only *for*', their characters, a strategy that augments our capacity to grasp that which we have not personally lived or experienced (2016: 39, italics in original). In fact, it seems counterintuitive that a scene like the possession dance in Luca Guadagnino's remake of *Suspiria* (2018), in which a female dancer's body is contorted to death via psychic projection, would generate anything other than extreme apprehension and sympathy for the sufferer.

Competition sports and coming-of-age travails are the specific remit of feminist body horror because both are corporeally fixated and propped up by the entreaties of those who supervise and control the protagonists. At a time when teenage girls are particularly vulnerable to social media's influence on self-perception – the messages and advice shared by online models and the opportunities and demands that come from peer comparison and feedback (Casares and Binkley, 2022; Choukas-Bradley et al., 2022) – it is not surprising that texts have leaned heavily on its impacts on body image. For instance, *Hatching* (Hanna Bergholm, 2022) centres on the impositions made on twelve-year-old Tinja (Siiri Solalinna) by her mother, a former figure skater-turned-influencer who monetises her family for content creation and who insists on projecting a manufactured picture-perfect fantasy of middle-class pulchritude and overachievement. Tinja is forced to compete in gymnastics at professional levels, something that devolves into painful injuries and dissatisfaction. Tinja's pent-up repression takes the form of yet another feral double, this time an untameable birdlike creature of destruction she rescues from a dying crow and nurtures to full growth. Tinja's doppelgänger resembles her but embodies everything that the mother's manicured, carefully curated version of reality filters out: the rebelliousness, unkemptness and confusion of adolescence (Figure 26). *Cam* (Daniel Goldhaber, 2018) also takes issue with the schizoid nature of online interactions. Although at first glance a diametrically opposite film, focusing as it does on the online pornography industry, its conclusions are comparable. Alice (Madeline Brewer), a camgirl vying for attention in a crowded digital marketplace, fakes her own suicide to attract viewers and popularity. After this desperate move, a double, Lola, takes over her live-stream account with a lot more success. A final showdown between the girls sees Alice breaking her own nose in a desperate attempt to win a challenge that will make Lola vanish. *Cam*'s ending is less confident in its protagonist's ability to gain

Figure 26 In *Hatching*, Tinja's feral body double rebels against gendered expectations, represented by her mother.
Source: *Hatching*, directed by Hanna Bergholm (Sylva Mysterium Oy, 2022)

real independence from her doppelgänger. Alice's adoption of a new identity in a bid to restart her career suggests troublesome links between gender, sexuality and online activity. However empowered by the prospect of capitalising on their youth and desirability, the requirements of an exchange ruled by customers' projections of female fantasies take their toll on workers who must, to some degree, transform themselves and their bodies into objects of desire dependent on external approval and ratings. Only because this brand of biopower incorporates informed consent does not mean its basic structures are fundamentally revised. Social media and online content impose a confusing schism between the real self and its idealised image (the 'filtered' self) that body horror's supernatural register takes apart.

It is significant that many of the texts considered thus far have been either directed or written by women. Body horror has grown exponentially as a result of authorial intent and raised awareness that, in Joyce Carol Oates's words, the subgenre 'in its myriad manifestations speaks most powerfully to women and girls' (2023: 2). New voices have endeavoured to revitalise the figure of the monstrous-feminine in ways that respond to modern conceptualisations of feminism. The body in feminist horror is so vast and varied that it resists generalisation, yet it is fair to propose that underpinning the subgenre lies a concerted effort to transfer monstrosity and shame away from female bodies and onto patriarchal powers, the medical, legal and economic tendrils of which have historically held control. If many of these texts engage with familiar concerns because these have sadly not disappeared, they do not necessarily condone or reify female monstrosity. A correlative has been the re-emergence of the 'gaslight' Gothic submode of Charlotte Brontë's *Jane Eyre* (1847) and Daphne du Maurier's *Rebecca* (1938) in texts like Carmen Maria Machado's short story 'The Husband Stitch' (2014) and the films *Swallow* (Carlo Mirabella-Davis, 2019), *Crimson Peak* (Guillermo del Toro, 2015) and *The Invisible Man* (Leigh Whannell, 2020), where the antagonist is a Byronic husband.[44] Such texts bespeak the advent of fourth-wave feminism and rise of gender activism around systemic inequalities and the denouncing of the pervasiveness of rape culture. A phrase coined in 2006, 'Me Too', coalesced into a social movement around 2017, when the #MeToo hashtag went viral following Harvey Weinstein's multiple accusations of sexual abuse. As an empowering awareness campaign, one of its main goals is to share experiences of sexual abuse and harassment, helping give them visibility and build critical mass around the need for real solutions. Mariana Enríquez's short story 'Things We Lost in the Fire' (2016) captures the spirit of such contemporary feminist protest at its most uncompromising and in stark body horror terms. Enríquez flips the script on domestic violence (acid attacks) and femicide by having women wil-fully burn their faces and bodies. As one of the characters explains, as extreme as the act may sound, it works to some degree: suddenly 'there's no more prostitution' (Enríquez, 2017: 197). Violence is repurposed as political weapon in many contemporary feminist body horror texts to denounce gender inequalities and sexist exploitation.

3.2 Queer Body Horror

Body horror's natural interests in the boundaries between bodies and their social imprinting have also made it a receptacle for queer anxieties and fantasies of liberation. Academic studies have carefully scrutinised the representational relevance of mainstream horror from a queer perspective: the patterns of extreme alterity exhibited by the monster – its outlandishness and embodiment of that which heteronormativity and patriarchy render 'other' or, even worse, deviant, diseased, sinful and evil – can be traced to the medical, judicial and religious models of exclusion that have abjected, where not criminalised, queer subjects due to their perceived difference, 'abnormality' and, especially after the AIDS crisis, infectiousness.[45] Horror film has evolved dramatically from the days when queer desire could only be obliquely referenced or intimated in films

---

[44] These texts offer variations on the formula, which they do not follow slavishly but rather use as a starting point.

[45] See Benshoff (1997).

like *Dracula's Daughter* (Lambert Hillyer, 1936), *The Haunting* (Robert Wise, 1963), *The Lost Boys* (Joel Schumacher, 1987), *Nightbreed* (Clive Barker, 1990) or *Interview with the Vampire* (Neil Jordan, 1994).[46] Openly queer horror cinema, television and literature, with 'out' characters that make symbolic readings of the monster redundant, have striven to break with a tradition that, regardless of its sometimes comforting catalysis of exclusion and trauma, can also act as a pathologising mirror that continues to paint the exceptional as villainous or essentially wretched. New queer horror is therefore characterised by the centring of queer subjectivity in all its gendered and sexual complexity, highlighting mental health and personal crises, from self-acceptance and 'coming out' journeys to the compromises of assimilation and conflicts between communities and LGBTQIA+ subcultures.[47] Although external monsters, typically in the shape of hateful bigots who wish protagonists harm, have not gone away, it is definitely possible to trace an inwards psychological journey in twenty-first-century queer horror narratives, as well as a complication of neat sexual and gender categories. Body horror has played an important part in reproducing some of these concerns.

As plural and fluid as queer identities have proven to be, they are still today largely refracted by common, or at least similar, instances of marginalisation and isolation caused by their minoritarian status. Arguably, these shared experiences of exclusion and disempowerment are simultaneously what enable LGBTQIA+ people to rally together to demand political and social change. For many, growing up gay, bi, non-binary or trans (among other sexualities and genders on the queer spectrum) is hard, even impossible, due to external heteronormative pressures that force us to perform and present in ways that align our biological sex with traditional notions of gender and their corresponding sexual correlatives from the moment we are born.[48] Reprisal for failing to comply with these conventions can manifest as behavioural correctives (disapproving looks, gentle chiding and discouragement) or, in increasing levels of violence, verbal threats, physical attacks and murder. This policing of queerness is compounded by its visibility, since queerness can be corporeally inscribed (effeminacy, butchness, sartorial choices) or deducible from certain practices or actions (holding hands, kissing in public, mannerisms). External vigilance in turn breeds an internalisation of the discriminatory discourse used against queer

---

[46] The 1960s, 1970s and 1980s saw an influx of lesbian vampires in countries like Spain, France and Italy, where monsters were able to channel otherwise forbidden or 'evil' sexual behaviours. The progressiveness of these representations is somewhat curtailed by their exploitative titillation.

[47] See Elliott-Smith (2016), Westengard (2019), Elliott-Smith and Browning (2020), Haefele-Thomas (2023) and Ollett (2024).

[48] Sometimes gendering happens even before birth, as with gender reveal parties.

people, leading to feelings of shame or internalised homophobia and a hyperawareness of gendered and sexual codings. Fear of being outed or negative feelings about one's own body due to sexological and gendered expectations also affect the interrelations between the external/internal and the social/personal. For some queer people, there is a sense that gender is also something that can be performed incorrectly and even deliberately against the grain, acts that are personal but also fundamentally public because their impact on the self and on society depends on them being comprehended by others as compliant or dissident, normative or exceptional.

Horror can be more than a reflective lens, and when queer-themed and especially when queer-authored, truly expansive and meticulous in its analysis of difficult, sometimes paradoxical feelings, as well as of bonds that extend beyond the biological family. Queer body horror has a penchant for change and growth, emphasising the importance of difference, and above all, its acceptance, enabling us to rewrite our lives, to understand ourselves as fluid subjects in transition. In Julia Armfield's novel *Our Wives Under the Sea*, a meditation on grief and loss, readers follow the parallel narratives of Leah, a deep-sea researcher who starts to turn into a fish-like creature following a six-month expedition gone wrong, and Miri, her wife. The ending, in which Miri surrenders Leah to '[t]his alchemist sea, changing something into something else' (Armfield, 2022: 228), having come to terms with her partner's fundamental transformation, demonstrates the desire to do right by Leah irrespective of direct comprehensibility of her new ontological state. In *Sick Girl* (Lucky McKee, 2006), a short film in the first season of the *Masters of Horror* series (2005–2007), an exotic insect mediates the relationship between shy entomologist Ida (Angela Bettis) and girl-next-door Misty (Erin Brown), even performing the role of metaphorical inseminator. At the end, horror is partially relinquished in favour of a sweet moment of maternal bliss, as both women sit content together and wonder who will give birth first (Figure 27). And in Jade Song's *Chlorine* (2023), about a teenage girl who wants to become a mermaid, destiny trumps the pain of becoming and is equated with 'transcendence' and 'free[dom]' (2023: 218, 220).

Queer body horror, with its fascination with speculative forms of corporeality and change, is also particularly interested in notions of intimacy, especially in the digital age. As critics like Stephen Marche have warned, the era of the smartphone (introduced in 2008) and of social media – the 'ephemerality' and 'facelessness' associated with both – has led to a strange scenario in which 'the sharing of private experience has never been more widespread while empathy, the ability to recognize the meaning of another's private experience, has never been more rare' (2024). Marche also writes about rising numbers of individuals

Figure 27 Lesbian connection and conception are facilitated by a strange
bug in *Sick Girl*.
Source: *Sick Girl* (S1 E10), directed by Lucky McKee, *Masters of Horror* (Showtime,
2006)

suffering from loneliness and narcissism and of a noticeable decline in political
solidarity. While telecommunications technology itself may not be the root of
the problem and can be framed as an escalation of the capitalist maxims that
promulgate an 'openly connected' society, 'the exploitation of intimate connections for marketing purposes, intimacy exhibitionism and breaches of privacy'
(Chambers, 2017: 34, 33) does point towards a crisis of intimacy. Digital media
has enabled the valorisation of certain bodies through platforms like Instagram,
YouTube and TikTok that trade in likes and views and more literally in porno-
graphic subscription channels like OnlyFans that charge a fee for access to
explicit 'personal' material. All these social networking sites give the illusion of
closeness and unmediated contact with people we are unlikely to know or meet
in real life. A partisan reading of these cultural developments would argue that
the current situation is directly proportional to the competitive individualism
underlying digital capitalism and that such image and video platforms have also
created collective attachments.[49] For example, social media and dating apps
have allowed LGBTQIA+ people to meet each other beyond the relatively safe
spaces of specialised pubs and venues. Queer body horror probes the grey area
between an optimistic and pessimistic view of queer bonding in the internet age,
and this is visible in the very fabric of new fictions.

---

[49] See Hakin (2020).

The bulk of Eric LaRocca's novella *Things Have Gotten Worse Since We Last Spoke* (2022) is composed of the communications, mostly exchanged emails and instant messages, between the deceased Agnes Petrella, a seller in a queer community board, and Zoe Cross, who initiates a relationship with her. LaRocca's novella investigates power imbalances in romantic attachments, with Agnes falling into the role of a submissive, and Zoe of a dominant looking 'for a woman to belong to [her]', '[s]omebody who answers only to [her], as if [she] was the hand of God that feeds them' (2022: 64). Initial dares aimed at helping Agnes 'mak[e] colossal strides toward the ownership of [her] true identity – a fearless young woman' (57) take a darker turn when Zoe drafts a contract establishing a master/slave relationship between the two that grants her complete ownership and control. The twist is that Zoe's demands for gross tests of faith and blind trust become less worrying than Agnes's dependence and self-destructive tendencies, which culminate in a planned infection by tapeworm – a token of her lover and the life they create together – and her eventual suicide. The motif of the tapeworm is also used in Alison Rumfitt's *Brainwyrms* (2023), where non-binary Vanya joins an online forum for '*people who [are] sexually excited by the idea of parasites*' (2023: 154, italics in original), who want to nurture them or give them to others. Beyond its capacity as niche kink connected to teenage sexual curiosity and the novel's overarching themes of infertility and impregnation fetishes, the tapeworm Vanya contracts symbolises their desire for intimacy and understanding, as well as a nihilistic confusion stemming from personal trauma. As a queer teenager damaged by abusive parenting and a survivor of sibling rape, Vanya craves real connections (being listened to, being cared for) and 'the closest form of intimacy' (225). The death of the tapeworm, a parasitic life form that only takes and gives nothing back, marks Vanya's awareness of toxic relationships, of the need for commitment in love.

Body horror can invoke more precise social issues that plague queer people in particular. For instance, Alice Maio Mackay's playful *T-Blockers* (2023) returns to the trope of contagion to parody contemporary social outcries about hormonal treatments in trans adolescents and transphobic tirades that have equated the surge of medical referrals to an 'epidemic'.[50] The parasitic worms in this film transform people into murderous queer bashers instead, offering a commentary on the virulence of transphobic hate (Figure 28). The script even hints at a certain indeterminacy between those whose volition is overridden by the supernatural bugs and the town's everyday 'skinhead[s]', 'incel[s]' and anti-trans rights rally protesters bent on fighting 'all things believed to be different and unusual'. Equally, *Swallowed* (Carter Smith, 2022), about two men who are

---

[50] See Allegretti (2024).

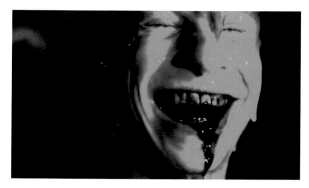

Figure 28 Parasitic infection acts as metaphor for virulent transphobia in
T-Blockers.
Source: *T-Blockers*, directed by Alice Maio Mackay (One Manner Productions, 2023)

forced to smuggle hallucinogenic larvae inside their bodies, seems to tackle the thorny issue of drugs on the gay scene. The bite of the poisonous insects has a couple of significant side effects; they can help one maintain an erection for hours and enhance sexual feeling at the expense of immobility, qualities that echo actual recreational substances associated with chemsex parties, such as GHB/GBL, mephedrone, crystal meth, cocaine or ketamine. And in Gretchen Felker-Martin's novel *Manhunt* (2022), a text that captures the transgressive attitude of 1980s 'splatterpunk', a familiar post-apocalyptic scenario of scant resources and survivor strife literalises the conflict that has come to be known as the 'TERF wars'.[51] Trans women Fran and Beth roam around a ravaged US coast, fending off attacks from TERF soldiers and cisgender men, who have grown feral from a virus targeting anyone with high levels of testosterone. In this scenario, external harm is just as worrying as internal hormonal changes that would compromise a person's integrity. '*[I]f I ever run out of spiro and E I'll be one of them a few weeks later*' (Felker-Martin, 2022: 6, italics in original), laments one of the protagonists, straight after harvesting raw testicles, one of the last remaining sources of oestrogen in this fallen world. The body horror in *Manhunt* is incredibly politicised, a reflection on the public condemnation of hormone replacement therapy as well as the medical diagnosis ('gender dysphoria') necessary to obtain access to treatment.[52] For some trans thinkers, like philosopher Paul B. Preciado, the workings of this psychiatric

---

[51] TERF stands for 'trans-exclusionary radical feminism', a form of gender-critical feminism that has clashed with trans rights activists. The TERF wars gained momentum in 2017 in the UK as a result of the Tory party's plans to reform the Gender Recognition Act 2004 (Pearce et al., 2020).

[52] At least this is the case at the time of writing.

category represent biopower at its finest, a requirement tantamount to a forced declaration of 'madness' that demands the acknowledgement of a 'distance' between body and mind that might not actually be felt as such by the individual (2022: 17, my translation).

Like gay and lesbian horror, which has taken a long time to establish itself as a weighty category of entertainment due to its supposed sectionalised appeal and alignment with 'camp' cinema, trans horror is a relative novelty in audio-visual media, despite the digital release of trans slasher *They/Them* (John Logan) in 2022. Trans characters, like gay and lesbian ones, have rarely appeared in canonical examples of the horror genre and even more seldom as anything other than negative, transphobic stereotypes like evil killers, sex workers, deceivers or dead fodder.[53] In films like *Dressed to Kill* (Brian De Palma, 1980), *Sleepaway Camp* (Robert Hiltzik, 1983) and *The Silence of the Lambs* (Jonathan Demme, 1991), and in the wake of Alfred Hitchcock's *Psycho*, trans villains were presented as homicidal cross-dressers played by cisgender actors. The rise of trans horror is recent because it belongs to a broader opening up of industries (television and cinema) that have been traditionally conservative in terms of representation and inclusion, and which began gaining momentum and critical mass towards the end of the 2010s. Actors like Laverne Cox, Hunter Schaefer, Hari Nef, Elliot Page, Michaela Jae, Indya Moore, Zión Moreno and Miss Benny have played likeable leads in films and shows that are driving change in social perceptions. Increasing numbers of transgender and non-binary directors like Rhys Ernst, Silas Howard, Isabel Sandoval, Janet Mock, Sam Feder, Yance Ford and the Wachowskis mean that trans identities, in all their complexities, are being centred and written about by members of those communities. Representation of trans characters has likewise grown in horror, with films like *Hellraiser* (David Bruckner, 2022) and *Talk to Me* featuring trans actors in prominent roles, and artists like Jane Schoenbrun, Our Lady J, Louise Weard and M. J. Bassett directing and scripting horror. Being less constrained by big budgets and studio backing and more supportive of creative autonomy, literature has been even more forthcoming, with Gothic, Weird and horror writers such as Rivers Solomon and Caitlín R. Kiernan producing important texts. Just as vital as access to distribution markets for artists is the fact that new narratives are trans-led and trans-affirming.

The connection between transness and body horror is akin to, but also fundamentally different from, that of its gay and lesbian cousin. Biopolitical

---

[53] Dr Frank-N-Furter, played by Tim Curry in *The Rocky Horror Picture Show* (Jim Sharman, 1975), is one of the few exceptions.

processes of gender and sexual regulation via familial, public and medico-legal scrutiny are more pronounced in trans and non-binary cases, where biology does not align with or debunks the dyadic gender model and where chromosomal boundaries may be crossed via hormonal treatments or puberty blockers. Trans people also have to contend with cissexism, oppositional sexism and, in the case of trans women, trans-misogyny.[54] Ongoing debates about allowing or banning transgender, especially transfeminine, people from using public facilities that align with their gender identity have tended to focus on biologically essentialist claims that trans-inclusive practices could lead to sexual attacks on women and children.[55] Other public debates about the irreversible effects of hormonal treatments and gender-affirming surgery or the association of teenage anxiety and depression with transness attest to the forensic speculation over trans identity.[56] Body horror speaks to the uncertainties and vulnerabilities of living in a body that is subjected to the majoritarian–minoritarian control imbalances of cisgender, heteronormative biopower, but also to internal struggles like feelings of dispossession and disidentification with one's own body or the need to be seen and acknowledged by others as one sees oneself. For trans people who undergo surgical procedures to feminise or masculinise their appearance, there is the additional worry that these could go wrong or not be as effective as expected. Trans body horror collects many of these worries, sometimes using supernatural phenomena to effect sex changes, as in the short stories 'Fencing Breastplate' (2022), by Avi Burton, and 'Chironoplasty' (2022), by Joe Koch, but usually pushes for self-acceptance and resistance to external pressure.[57] For instance, in Eve Harms's *Transmuted* (2021), Isa undergoes an '[e]*xperimental feminization treatment for trans women*' (23, italics in original) that goes horribly wrong and eventually turns her into a monster. Yet the novella ends with an assertive self-questioning – 'What's the point of hiding? . . . Why am I afraid to be seen by strangers who mean nothing to me? Why should I be scared for my family to find out what I look like?' (98) – and with Isa bod modding in a successful bid to reclaim ownership of her body.

Trans body horror is generally positive about transformations, no doubt due to its appreciation of fluidity and suspicion of oppositional sex and gender categories. In fact, trans body horror, like trans theory more broadly, has celebrated the 'mutant' category and even reclaimed it as an empowering metaphor. In his treatise *Can the Monster Speak?* (2023 [2020]), Preciado (Figure 29), who self-administered testosterone for a number of years and

---

[54] See Serano (2016).   [55] See, for example, Anonymous (2020).
[56] See Barnes (2023) and Roush (2024).
[57] Both stories can be found in Woodroe and Blairstone (2022).

Figure 29 Trans philosopher Paul B. Preciado has embraced the 'mutant' as positive and transitional metaphor.

Source: Sebastian Reuter / Stringer / Getty Images Entertainment / Getty Images

who has since become one of the most important trans figures of the early twenty-first century, writes of the embrace of his 'condition as monster' and his preference for this descriptor over 'that of man or woman' because '[t]he monster is one who lives in transition. One whose face, body and behaviours cannot yet be considered true in a predetermined regime of power and knowledge' (35). In the introduction to the collection *An Apartment in Uranus* (2023 [2019]), he elaborates: 'To be trans is . . . to accept that one can only arrive at oneself thanks to change, to mutation, to hybridisation' (43). Many trans body horror texts reflect this conception of the self as ever-changing and remaking itself, and go as far as to refashion alterity as a desirable goal. Whether that is becoming worm, mushroom or fleshy virus-spreading creature – in LC von Hessen's 'Wormspace' (2023), Derek Des Agnes's 'Coming Out' (2023) and Layne Van Rensburg's 'Long Fingers' (2023), respectively – transformation is equated with growth, acceptance and resistance to normative assimilation, formulated as an invitation to stand out and treasure abjection as proof of uniqueness and honesty.[58] In Hailey Piper's *Queen of Teeth* (2021), a Weird

---

[58] These stories can be found in Gislason (2023).

novel about Yaya, a woman who grows teeth in her vagina as a result of pharmaceutical experiments, body horror leads not to a tale of destruction, decay and disintegration, but to one of incorporation (of other bodies into an indefinite organic biomass). By the end, Magenta, the 'monster' who starts off as a parasite yet eventually merges with and absorbs Yaya, has destroyed the evil corporation and regained her lover. Doc, transformed by the experience, sees the present 'as a miasma of endless feeling and unstoppable bliss' (Piper, 2021: 195). The undefinable, unpindownable body escapes the prison of signification and becomes a source of comfort, trust, love and zest for life.

3.3 Black Body Horror

When she coined the term 'Black horror' in 2011, little could scholar Robin R. Means Coleman have predicted that the commercial and critical success of *Get Out* (Jordan Peele, 2017) would shortly after revolutionise horror, contributing to its politicisation and initiating a new wave of genre films directed and scripted by African American directors.[59] For her, Black horror is not defined by the appearance of Black characters, but rather by the fact that its examples are '"race" films': 'they have an added narrative focus that calls attention to racial identity, in this case Blackness – Black culture, history, ideologies, experiences, politics, language, humour, aesthetics, style, music, and the like' (Coleman, 2011: 7). Black horror centres Black experience, authorially and representationally, so it is natural that, while it would continue to draw on traditional horror strategies, scenarios, tropes and motifs, it would also develop its own unique set of parameters. Naturally, Black horror is a broad church encompassing a variety of texts and sociopolitical anxieties, some of them more concerned with internal community dynamics, religious and spiritual themes or gender and sexuality, but broadly speaking, Black horror has been understood to reflect the experience of 'living in a country built on white supremacy', the United States, where 'race … informs every aspect of life', and thus 'address[es] social – primarily race-related issues' (Coleman and Harris, 2023: 92).[60] Fear may sparingly manifest within African American communities, for instance in the in-depth questioning of what 'Blackness' means to various individuals in *The Blackening* (Tim Story, 2022). Still the monster typically remains white privilege and social injustice.

The ideological concerns of Black horror bear out in many of the films that have come to be associated with the subgenre and have explored the various social spheres that (re)produce discrimination and operate on basic racist

---

[59] Dawn Keetley's edited collection on the film explicitly names it 'political horror' (2020).

[60] Black horror is a global cultural manifestation that extends beyond the US. Due to spatial constraints, I am limiting the scope to US-made Black horror here, but see Coleman and Lawrence (2024) for the bigger picture.

principles. For example, *Master* (Mariama Diallo, 2022) targets educational diversity policies in Higher Education, *Body Cam* (Malik Vitthal, 2020) the police force and *Nope* (Jordan Peele, 2022) cinema as cultural and representational institution. In *Antebellum* (Gerard Bush and Christopher Renz, 2020), a film reminiscent of Octavia E. Butler's novel *Kindred* (1979), a direct thread is woven between past and present when the horrors of the plantation are shown to be very much alive in a contemporary Civil War re-enactment park.[61] Similarly, texts like the first season of *Them* (2021), created by Little Marvin, set their action in periods still governed by segregation to capture its effects on the minds of Black characters. The supernatural has been used to symbolise trauma, oppression and prejudice, especially in the fiction of Toni Morrison, Nalo Hopkinson and Butler, yet given the material reality of white supremacy and racism, ghosts sometimes become redundant figures in contemporary Black horror. Pointing the finger at the history of medical experimentation on African Americans, *The First Purge* (Gerard McMurray, 2018), about a governmental experiment to 'purge' Staten Island of those who do not have the money or means to defend themselves against state-sanctioned crime (the racialised and destitute), plays like Trump-era social realism, with a scene recalling the 2017 Charlottesville 'Unite the Right' rally.

The fact that protagonists in Black horror are African American means that Black bodies are under attack and that these texts necessarily investigate, consciously or not, the intimate relationships between corporeality, identity, race, politics and the law, as well as the distance between subjectivity and external perception. Placing the emphasis on the Black Lives Matter movement that gained international attention following global protests against the murder of George Floyd in 2020 (Figure 30), Maisha Wester understands the cultural work of contemporary Black horror as exposing the disenfranchisement and criminalisation of Black people, 'working to record and demystify the sociopolitical forces dooming Black life to vicious bio- and necropolitics' (2023: 173). Although there is no specific 'Black body horror' variant, it is possible to suggest that all Black horror incorporates some elements of body horror when understood at its most essential and visceral. My preoccupation thus far has been the type of horror that stages dilemmas through corporeal transformation or transmutation and, while Black horror is, with good reason, less hopeful than feminist or queer body horror, it is possible to find in it examples of rejection and resistance that materialise as a redemptive, collective body with the potential to bring about change and encourage an empowering sense of community.

---

[61] The film begins as an apparently historical film. However, the ending reveals the action to be set in the present day, where a Senator is trying to re-impose chattel slavery.

Figure 30 Black body horror has been directly influenced by anti-racist activism like the Black Lives Matter movement.
Source: Bryan R. Smith / Contributor / AFP / Getty Images

Black body horror explores the specific interrelations between embodiment (the Black body as biological entity) and sociopolitical inscription (the Black body as legal, economic and aesthetic construct produced by colonial history and cultural mediation) in the constitution of 'Black personhood', or the 'constant interplay between the actual body of a racialised person and the representational schema that coalesce around that body' (Okoth, 2022: 228).

Get Out was a crucial film in critiquing the white liberalism of a supposedly post-racial America, the hypocrisy and bigotry of those that 'would have voted for Obama a third time' but who still objectify, stereotype, fetishise and exceptionalise Black people. The body of protagonist Chris (Daniel Kaluuya) is the subject of verbal micro-aggressions – like comments on his physical appearance and genetic prowess – and eventually the object sold at a 'body' auction that echoes the slave trade. The film's conceit, reminiscent of the body swaps in Ira Levin's novel *The Stepford Wives* (1972), is that a wealthy white elite have attained immortality by having their ageing brains transplanted into Black individuals, whose physical attributes they favour. The hosts become mere passengers in the Sunken Place, a 'psychological oubliette ... where [Black people] [a]re stripped of all agency and left alone with [their] struggle' (Peele, 2023: viii), conscious but otherwise unable to control their actions. Literalising the idea of the Black body as white possession, *Get Out* also establishes a dialectic between physical and psychological entrapment that gains meaning through Chris's profession as a photographer specialising in deprived urban landscapes. As he would do again in *Nope*, Peele seems concerned with the specular logic of mediation: how representations of Black people, or their scarcity, can end up reflecting and constructing identity. Such a dynamic is particularly damaging when not carried out by Black artists who can subvert or disrupt the intrinsic power structures and hierarchies of the normative, majoritarian gaze, as it fixes ways of looking and being looked at that are not balanced or equitable and can even encourage dissociative effects. *Get Out* makes a case for the need to fight harmful portrayals in visual media because, in the American context, these also have a necropolitical history in the consumption of Black pain, from lynchings to police brutality and the struggle for freedom (Okoth, 2022: 235). Although the cinematic shape the Sunken Place takes for Chris channels the specifics of his childhood trauma (his mother died while he sat paralysed in front of the television), it is difficult not to read it as a metaphor for the stasis of the audiovisual practices that have framed the Black body in American popular culture and continued the ideological work of colonialism and racial oppression (Figure 31).

Body horror, like speculative fiction, has the ability to move past social realism to reflect on power racial structures metaphorically. In 'Strange Case', the fifth episode of Misha Green's series *Lovecraft Country* (2020), a Dr Jekyll and Mr Hyde-style potion provides willing takers with the ability to become temporarily white. In the original Matt Ruff novel, the elixir is framed as panacea, offering Ruby 'the freedom to choose [her] own destiny' (2018: 224) and overcome the limitations she has experienced as a Black woman living in mid-1950s New England. Ruby, played in the series by Wunmi Mosaku, is suddenly able to aspire to jobs formerly barred to her, such as department store manager. Yet the change brings with it a concomitant identity crisis of misrecognition that initiates the 'body horror', for the 'other' here is a distillation of white privilege. 'Strange Case' thus argues that white freedoms are inextricable from the inequalities, hierarchies and histories of violence and oppression they are built upon. Ruby's ideological infection is illustrated by the scene where she feels the urge to aggressively remind Tamara (Sibongile Mlambo), a Black retail associate, that she needs to be 'exponentially better' than white people 'if she is to be a credit to [her] race'. *Lovecraft Country* turns its attention to the connections between body and society, to how corporeality and identity are economically and politically determined outside of the subject. The fact that Ruby never stops being fully herself blurs the lines between her and 'Hillary' (her white persona), suggesting that what has taken place is not a complete transformation or 'death' of the self. This is significant, for it encapsulates the journey towards the self–other.

Figure 31 The view from the Sunken Place in *Get Out* resembles
a cinema or television screen.

Source: *Get Out*, directed by Jordan Peele (Blumhouse Productions, QC Entertainment
and Monkeypaw Productions, 2017)

Ruby's metamorphoses are visceral and traumatic, her 'return' a markedly
carnal and bloody rebirth in which one woman emerges from inside the other. At
first, Ruby thinks she might have to perish to turn into Hillary and describes the
process as 'being unmade' – statements that heighten how her sense of self
originates in her embodied personhood. When another character, Christina
(Abbey Lee), discloses that she has been imbibing a similar elixir to transform
herself into a man so as to overcome the constraints imposed on her as a woman,
the series explicitly renders whiteness and maleness historically constructed
objects of oppression and desire. That Ruby eventually embraces 'magic' more
generally but gives up on the elixir is relevant too. She finds an assertive sense
of agency and comes to terms with her personal needs, but this celebration does
not entail a radical ontological change, merely an opening up. 'You can't relate

to who I am', declares Ruby impatiently when Christina purports to understand her predicament, but in the later episode 'Jig-a-Bobo' (S1 E8), she eventually begs her to 'feel what [she] feels'. Black body horror, like other forms of progressive body horror, does not merely gesture at the economic and structural inequalities between bodies (racialised and gendered). It proposes that a real sense of empathy can emerge from the creative process of embracing the unrelatable, of putting oneself in somebody else's shoes and learning from their struggles. As the storyline advances towards a 'BIPOC alternative life-world', a 'vision of collective self-care' (Shapiro, 2021) surfaces.

The empathic project is abstracted into a collective Black body in Nia DaCosta's *Candyman* (2021). Both continuing and re-imagining Bernard Rose's 1992 film of the same title, *Candyman* tells the story of Anthony (Yahya Abdul-Mateen II), a painter who finds inspiration in the fate of the Cabrini-Green projects, a 1970s racialised space 'with a particularly bad reputation' once left to moulder and later gentrified. Fieldwork leads him to find out about the Candyman, an urban legend about a man with a hook for a hand who can be summoned by saying his name in front of a mirror five times – with fatal consequences for the invoker. His fascination with Cabrini-Green (its past and fate) ignites a creative phase that sees him produce a series of macabre, Baconesque portraits of what is eventually implied are murdered Black men. Symbolically, these portraits are painted with a hand that is stung by a bee on the day Anthony learns about the Candyman. The necrotic decay that begins in that appendage and eventually extends to Anthony's arm, neck and face is tellingly shaped like the combs in a hive (Figure 32). Bees are proxy insects for the Candyman, and not just because they were used to torture Daniel Robitaille

Figure 32 Anthony's body grows honeycomb indentations as he becomes 'hive' in *Candyman*.

Source: *Candyman*, directed by Nia DaCosta (Universal Pictures and Metro-Goldwyn-Mayer, 2021)

(Tony Todd), the first in the spectral line. Bees live in colonies where individuals coordinate, cooperate and protect each other, a behaviour that instantiated the term 'hive mind' to name a notional thinking group. In learning about the Candyman and his story, Anthony eventually becomes him, a transformation signalled early on by mirrors that return the image of Sherman Fields (Michael Hargrove), an innocent Black man mistaken for a criminal and shot dead by the police. His metamorphosis into one of the swarm's many faces is completed by his copycat death, described as a 'sacrament' by another character.

Candyman has an underlying narrative – William Burke (Colman Domingo), traumatised by the violent death of Sherman and his return as the Candyman, aims to summon the ghost to dispense retributive vengeance against the gentrifying forces of Cabrini-Green – but the film works best as an allegorical musing on the need to draw attention to the victims of systemic racism and racial injustice. Its 'say his name' exhortation is a reference to the 2014 #SayHerName movement that arose in response to Black female victims of police and anti-Black brutality and subsequent 'Say Their Names' campaign. Candyman is described throughout as a multitude: a tape by sociology grad student Helen speaks of the Cabrini-Green myth as 'a survival tool' that 'grew from the community's collective subconscious'; an art critic talks of 'a ghost manifested by collective storytelling'; and William retorts that 'Candyman ain't a he, he's the whole damn hive'. He is also rationalised by characters into conceptual metaphors, such as a 'pain that lasts forever' and as 'how we deal with the fact that these things happened. That they're still happening', both references to the killing of African Americans. Upon his death, Anthony transmutes yet again from socially aware individual painter to synergistic, cumulative spirit. The Candyman's last words, 'tell every-one', echo Anthony's own when spelling his intention to 'spread the word', a phrase further politicised by the citational shadow puppet credits, where real twentieth-century victims of anti-Black violence like George Stinney or James Byrd Jr join the swarm. The body horror in *Candyman* is not particularly optimistic, mired as it is in the despair of what is presented as a time loop of violence, but it finds value and meaning in declaiming once occluded and still ignored systems of racist oppression. It insists upon a refusal of official messages, sublimates pain through supernatural vengeance and underscores the message that survival is a shared and mutual endeavour.

Through a coruscating indictment of the exploitative nature of capitalist structures, Boots Riley's satire *Sorry to Bother You* (2018) explicitly links the communal ethos of progressive body horror to the cooperative strength of trade unionism. In the film, down-on-his-luck Cash (LaKeith Stanfield) gets a job as a telemarketer for a big company, RegalView, where he thrives after learning to assume a 'white voice' that exudes confidence and self-assuredness. He is quickly promoted to 'Power Caller', a new exclusive role that involves working on a different floor and access to a much darker side of the business. He soon learns that WorryFree sells military arms and 'man power' (quickly rebranded 'slave labour', or onsite workers with no rights) to corporations who want to improve 'efficiency' and costs. Although Cash initially joins a workers union led by colleague Squeeze (Steven Yeun) and girlfriend Detroit (Tessa Thompson) reminds him of the historical relationship between slavery and capitalism, big money and the class mobility that it permits quickly destabilise his moral compass. *Sorry to Bother You* thus passes comment on what has come to be known as 'code-switching', 'a strategy for black people to successfully navigate interracial interactions' that 'has large implications for their well-being, economic advancement, and even physical survival' (McCluney et al., 2019). The film depicts both the benefits of 'downplaying membership in a stigmatized racial group' (perceived professionalism, increased likelihood of becoming a leader, promotion) and its downfalls (hostility from other in-group members, reduction of self-expression and burnout) (McCluney et al., 2019). Racial, class and economic allegiance grow almost indissoluble, particularly once the body horror element is introduced in the last third of the film.

At a party thrown by CEO Steve Lift (Armie Hammer), Cash is presented with a new company scheme to transform workers into horse–people hybrids, or 'Equisapiens'. As the shareholder promotional video explains, a 'chemical change' can make human labour, which 'has its limitations', 'stronger, more obedient, and therefore more efficient and profitable'. The simple and quick 'worker modification process' heralds the arrival of the future of labour, where productivity has been taken to its logical dehumanising endpoint and workers' capacity to fight back has been eradicated. The company's proposition to Cash is truly devious in its cruelty: he is to be planted in the new 'society' as a false leader in case of attempts at internal organisation or, as the CEO puts it, to be turned into an 'Equisapien Martin Luther King Jr' who represents the needs of WorryFree. When an outraged Cash denounces the company publicly, things backfire and the media and government hail the genetic advancement as a new 'scientific achievement'. Unionist zeal reawakened, Cash joins a strike, liberates the horse-people and, just as he muses on how great it is to be 'a part of something important – changing the world', he realises he too was infected with the fusing catalyst. The moment of existential body horror is short-lived, though, and dovetails into a final scene of group consolidation and activist battle.[62] The film concludes with a fully transformed Cash and his army of

---

[62] Collectivist underdog action is becoming a trope itself. In *Us* (Jordan Peele, 2019), the Tethered are genetic clones kept underground who eventually rebel against their 'surface' doubles and form a human chain reminiscent of the 1986 Hands Across America demonstration.

Figure 33 Body horror turns into horse-people revolution in
Sorry to Bother You.

Source: *Sorry to Bother You*, directed by Boots Riley (Cinereach, Macro, MNM
Creative, Significant Productions and The Space Program, 2018)

mutants breaking into the CEO's house as he reclaims the phrase 'sorry to
bother you', an apology that initially gave him up as 'not white enough' to make
money for the company (Figure 33).[63] In the ending of *Sorry to Bother You*,
Black horror's concerns with the socioeconomic inscription of Blackness com-
bine with body horror's militant spirit and desire for change.

4 Conclusion: Becoming Other(-)wise

A clear, if nuanced and intricate, picture emerges from even this brief consider-
ation of the new shapes and forms of body horror in the twenty-first century. As
many of the feminist, queer and anti-racist artists that have contributed to the
contemporary body horror canon confirm, this subgenre, like the horror genre
more broadly, has grown more personal and political than ever before, possibly
in part as a reaction to the rise of far-right threats and separatist policies in
Europe and of Trumpism in the US. A thorough emphasis on the transformative
potential of metamorphosis often counteracts with liberatory whimsy the exercises in disciplinarian power exhibited by texts seeking to expose the punitive
and hierarchical forces inherited from the patriarchal, colonial past. It is logical,
perhaps inevitable, that body horror will continue to become ever more de-
anchored from the parameters of specific genres, exceeding the barriers of
horror in search of speculative (un)realities that can voice the desires and
needs of new sociopolitical subjects endeavouring to deny or escape irreduc-
ibilities of sex, gender, sexuality and race. Where body horror continues to be

---

[63] The phrase 'not white enough' is uttered by Cash's colleague, Langston (Danny Glover).

particularly effective as fictional coding of real-world fears is in its exhibiting of the workings of the biopolitical construction of life, from the capitalist principles that determine what types of life are socially productive, worth living or even actually 'livable', as Judith Butler puts it (2004: 39), to the educational, familial, legal and medical structures of power that determine and even create available models of identity – gendered, sexual, racial, but also economic, religious and national.

Inherent to this process of discovery is the self-awareness awakened by our encounter with the 'other', which implies an ethical proximity to those inequalities we may not understand or even recognise due to given biases or privileges. Body horror's changes to the body, to personhood, encourage this move towards an enriching 'other' (a becoming 'other(-)wise', or wiser about the predicament of others, and 'otherwise', or different from ourselves) that can make us contemplate the world anew. Opening our eyes to biopolitical structures has benefits beyond promoting a richer, more ethical life. It can help us imagine ourselves according to parameters we may have unconsciously discarded or which have become normalised to the point of appearing common sense. Body horror constantly asks us to question everything: who makes the rules? Who benefits from them? What models of humanity and agency are thereby promoted? Who suffers? Who is erased? Part of this questioning leads to an inevitable dread: as the title of one of the collections studied in this book proposes, it is worth remembering that, despite neoliberal fictions of individuality and personal freedom, 'your body is not your body' (Woodroe and Blairstone, 2022). Bodies always exist and operate within fraught arenas – of what is acceptable, desirable, legal and commendable, and by contrast, of what is abject, discouraged, criminal or reprehensible. These models are still necessarily 'futurist' (Edelman, 2004: 12), based on exponential growth, profit and the primacy of states predominantly led by ideologies steeped in the colonial heteropatriarchy. The minoritarian has remained so due to repression from majoritarian forces that have tended towards hegemonic homogeny, extractive force and reproduction. Body horror, then, reminds us that our bodies ultimately belong to the states and social and economic systems within which they operate and that we are not who we think we are, or rather that being who we think we are is not free of ideological biases.

Crucially, we are simultaneously capable of thinking beyond current strictures: we can learn, we can change and we can collectivise; we can grow into morally aware individuals and communities that are able to perceive and fight injustices. As body horror makes clear, this sense of transformation is not just advantageous. Change is a fundamental constitutive part of being human, an evolutive inevitability and organic principle. Human language, key to many of the processes of agency and subjectivation covered in this book, works in this way too. It could be argued that body horror's transformative exercises, in their indulgence in what some may see as escapist fantasy, are limited in their impact. Is body horror ultimately found wanting against a context of rising sexism, homophobia, transphobia, racism and disablism? Is dissidence not still largely met with intimidatory strategies, where not downright punishment? Maybe so. But, as Paul B. Preciado posits, imagination is a crucial tool in registering the power of relational and transformational thinking. In fact, he sees it as the only way to overcome the extinction of life, which seems the de facto teleological end of 'the colonial techno-patriarchy' (2023a: 50). He hopes for a future in which 'we will manage to overcome racial epistemology and sexual difference and to invent a new cognitive framework allowing the existence of life's diversity' (51). Such a task is naturally a tall order for body horror alone, which emerges out of a wider milieu of representation and cultural production. And yet, a revolutionary fervour permeates the subgenre, inviting us to travel beyond the here and now. Body horror is an experiment in transitional configurations, of dead ends and new transcendental beginnings, of crossable borders and future possibilities.

References

Agamben, Giorgio, *Homo Sacer*: *Sovereign Power and Bare Life*, trans. Daniel Heller-Roazen (Stanford: Stanford University Press, 1998 [1995]).

Alaimo, Stacey, 'States of Suspension: Trans-Corporeality at Sea', *Interdisciplinary Studies in Literature and Environment* 19.3 (2012), 476–93.

Aldana Reyes, Xavier, 'Online Gothic', in Rebecca Duncan (ed.), *The Edinburgh Companion to Globalgothic* (Edinburgh: Edinburgh University Press, 2023), pp. 337–49.

Aldana Reyes, Xavier, 'Body Horror', in Stephen Shapiro and Mark Storey (eds.), *The Cambridge Companion to American Horror* (Cambridge: Cambridge University Press, 2022), pp. 107–19.

Aldana Reyes, Xavier, *Horror Film and Affect*: *Towards a Corporeal Model of Viewership* (New York: Routledge, 2016).

Aldana Reyes, Xavier, *Body Gothic*: *Corporeal Transgression in Contemporary Literature and Horror Film* (Cardiff: University of Wales Press, 2014).

Allegretti, Aubrey, 'Kemi Badenoch: "Epidemic" of Children Being Told They're Trans', *The Times*, 7 December 2023, www.thetimes.co.uk/article/schools-face-epidemic-of-children-told-theyre-transgender-badenoch-says-nch0kxkzp [last accessed 6 February 2024].

Anonymous, 'On the Policing of Toilets', *TransActual*, 14 June 2020, https://transactual.org.uk/blog/2020/06/14/on-the-policing-of-toilets/ [last accessed 8 February 2024].

Armfield, Julia, *Our Wives Under the Sea* (London: Picador, 2022).

Arnold, Sarah, *Maternal Horror Film*: *Melodrama and Motherhood* (Basingstoke: Palgrave Macmillan, 2013).

Asma, Stephen T., *On Monsters*: *An Unnatural History of Our Worst Fears* (Oxford: Oxford University Press, 2009).

Atkinson, Tiffany, 'Introduction', in Tiffany Atkinson (ed.), *The Body* (Basingstoke: Palgrave Macmillan, 2005), pp. 1–11.

Badley, Linda, *Writing Horror and the Body*: *The Fiction of Stephen King, Clive Barker and Anne Rice* (Westport: Greenwood Press, 1996).

Badley, Linda, *Film, Horror, and the Body Fantastic* (Westport: Greenwood Press, 1995).

Balanescu, Miriam, 'Gut Reaction: Cinema's New Wave of Projectile Vomiting', *The Guardian*, 13 April 2023, www.theguardian.com/film/2023/apr/13/gut-reaction-cinemas-new-wave-of-projectile-vomiting [last accessed 24 October 2023].

Barad, Karen, *Meeting the Universe Halfway: Quantum Physics and the Entanglement of Matter and Meaning* (Durham: Duke University Press, 2007).

Barnes, Hannah, 'Children on Puberty Blockers Saw Mental Health Change – New Analysis, *BBC News*, 19 September 2023, www.bbc.co.uk/news/health-66842352 [last accessed 8 February 2024].

Bazterrica, Agustina, *Tender Is the Flesh*, trans. Sarah Moses (London: Pushkin Press, 2020 [2017]).

Beard, William, 'Cronenberg, Flyness, and the Other-self', *Cinémas: Revue d'études cinématographiques*, 4.2 (1994): 153–72.

Benshoff, Harry M., *Monsters in the Closet: Homosexuality and the Horror Film* (Manchester: Manchester University Press, 1997).

Berkowitz, Dana, *Botox Nation: Changing the Face of America* (New York: New York University Press, 2017).

Blackman, Lisa, *The Body: The Key Concepts* (Oxford: Berg, 2008)

Blake, Linnie, '"Are We Worth Saving? You Tell Me": Neoliberalism, Zombies and the Failure of Free Trade', *Gothic Studies* 17.2 (2015): 26–41.

Bogle, Donald, *Toms, Coons, Mulattoes, Mammies, and Bucks: An Interpretive History of Blacks in American Films* (New York: Viking Press, 1973).

Botting, Fred, 'Zombie London: Unexceptionalities of the New World Order', in Lawrence Phillips and Anne Witchard (eds.), *London Gothic: Place, Space and the Gothic Imagination* (London: Continuum, 2010), pp. 153–71.

Bourgault du Coudray, Chantal, *The Curse of the Werewolf: Fantasy, Horror and the Beast Within* (London: I. B. Tauris, 2006).

Brophy, Philip, 'Horrality – The Textuality of Contemporary Horror Films', *Screen* 27.1 (1986): 2–13.

Brown, Jennifer, *Cannibalism in Literature and Film* (Basingstoke: Palgrave Macmillan, 2013).

Butler, Judith, *Undoing Gender* (New York: Routledge, 2004).

Carroll, Noël, *The Philosophy of Horror, or, Paradoxes of the Heart* (New York: Routledge, 1990).

Casares Jr., D. Robert, and Erin E. Binkley, 'An Unfiltered Look at Idealized Images: A Social Media Intervention for Adolescent Girls', *Journal of Creativity in Mental Health* 17.3 (2022): 313–31.

Chambers, Deborah, 'Networked Intimacy: Algorithmic Friendship and Scalable Sociality', *European Journal of Communication* 32.1 (2017): 26–36.

Choukas-Bradley, Sophia, Savannah R. Roberts, Anne J. Maheux, and Jacqueline Nesi, 'The Perfect Storm: A Developmental-Sociocultural Framework for the Role of Social Media in Adolescent Girls' Body Image Concerns and Mental Health', *Clinical Child and Family Psychology Review* 25 (2022): 681–701.

Christiansen, Steen Ledet, 'Pain and the Cinesthetic Subject in *Black Swan*', *Screen Bodies* 1.2 (2016): 25–41.

Clasen, Mathias, *Why Horror Seduces* (Oxford: Oxford University Press, 2017).

Colavito, Jason, *Knowing Fear: Science, Knowledge and the Development of the Horror Genre* (Jefferson: McFarland, 2008).

Coleman, Robin R. Means, *Horror Noire: Blacks in American Horror Films from the 1980s to the Present* (New York: Routledge, 2011).

Coleman, Robin R. Means, and Mark H. Harris, *The Black Guy Dies First: Black Horror Cinema from Fodder to Oscar* (New York: Saga Press, 2023).

Coleman, Robin R. Means, and Novotny Lawrence (eds.), *The Oxford Handbook of Black Horror Film* (Oxford: Oxford University Press, 2024).

Creed, Barbara, *The Monstrous-Feminine: Film, Feminism, Psychoanalysis* (Manchester: Manchester University Press, 1993).

Crenshaw, Kimberlé, 'Demarginalizing the Intersection of Race and Sex: A Black Feminist Critique of Antidiscrimination Doctrine, Feminist Theory and Antiracist Politics', *University of Chicago Legal Forum* 1.8 (1989): 139–67.

Cueva, Edmund P., *Horror in Classical Literature: 'On a Profound and Elementary Principle'* (Cardiff: University of Wales Press, 2024).

Cuthbertson, Anthony, 'Elon Musk Meets Congress Leader to Warn of AI Apocalypse', *The Independent*, 27 April 2023, www.independent.co.uk/tech/ elon-musk-ai-congress-schumer-b2327956.html [last accessed 14 November 2023].

D'Lacey, Joseph, *Meat* (London: Bloody Books, 2008).

Dearden, Nick, *Pharmanomics: How Big Pharma Destroys Global Health* (London: Verso, 2023).

Deleuze, Gilles, and Félix Guattari, *What Is Philosophy?*, trans. Hugh Tomlinson and Graham Burchell (New York: Columbia University Press, 2003 [1991]).

DeMello, Margo, *Body Studies: An Introduction* (New York: Routledge, 2014).

Doherty, Thomas, *Pre-Code Hollywood: Sex, Immorality, and Insurrection in American Cinema 1930–1934* (New York: Columbia University Press, 1999), pp. 347–67.

Douglas, Mary, *Purity and Danger: An Analysis of Concepts of Pollution and Taboo* (London: Routledge, 2009 [1966]).

Douglas, Mary, *Natural Symbols: Explorations in Cosmology* (New York: Routledge, 1978 [1970]).

Dyer, Richard, *White* (New York: Routledge, 1997).

Dymond, Erica Joan (ed.), *Grief in Contemporary Horror Cinema: Screening Loss* (Lanham: Lexington Books, 2022).

Edelman, Lee, *No Future*: *Queer Theory and the Death Drive* (Durham: Duke University Press, 2004).

Edwards, Justin D., Rune Graulund and Johan Höglund (eds.), *Dark Scenes from Damaged Earth*: *The Gothic Anthropocene* (Minneapolis: University of Minnesota Press, 2022).

Elliott-Smith, Darren, *Queer Horror Film and Television*: *Sexuality and Masculinity at the Margins* (London: I. B. Tauris, 2016).

Elliott-Smith, Darren, and John Edgar Browning (eds.), *New Queer Horror Film and Television* (Cardiff: University of Wales Press, 2020).

Enríquez, Mariana, *Things We Lost in the Fire*, trans. Megan McDowell (London: Granta, 2017 [2016]).

Esposito, Roberto, *Immunitas*: *The Protection and Negation of Life*, trans. Zakiya Hanafi (Cambridge: Polity, 2013 [2002]).

Falk, Pasi, *The Consuming Body* (London: SAGE, 1994).

Felker-Martin, Gretchen, *Manhunt* (New York: Nightfire, 2022).

Foster, Travis M., 'Introduction', in Travis M. Foster (ed.), *The Cambridge Companion to American Literature and the Body* (Cambridge: Cambridge University Press, 2022), pp. 1–10.

Foucault, Michel, '*Society Must Be Defended*': *Lectures at the Collège de France, 1975–76*, trans. David Macey (London: Penguin, 2004 [1997]).

Foucault, Michel, *The Will to Knowledge*: *The History of Sexuality, Vol. 1*, trans. Robert Hurley (London: Penguin, 1998 [1976]).

Friedman, Lester D., and Allison B. Kavey, *Monstrous Progeny*: *A History of the Frankenstein Narratives* (New Brunswick: Rutgers University Press, 2016).

Gamble, Christopher N., Joshua S. Hanan and Thomas Nail, 'What Is New Materialism?', *Angelaki*: *Journal of the Theoretical Humanities* 24.6 (2019): 111–34.

Giroux, Henry A., *Zombie Politics and Culture in the Age of Casino Capitalism* (Oxford: Peter Lang, 2011).

Gislason, Lor (ed.), *Bound in Flesh*: *An Anthology of Trans Body Horror* (San Antonio: Ghoulish Books, 2023).

Goldacre, Ben, *Bad Pharma*: *How Medicine Is Broken, and How We Can Fix It* (London: Fourth Estate, 2012).

Gonder, Patrick, 'Like a Monstrous Jigsaw Puzzle: Genetics and Race in Horror Films of the 1950s', *The Velvet Light Trap* 52 (2003): 33–44.

Goodbody, Axel, and Adeline Johns-Putra (eds.), *Cli-Fi*: *A Companion* (Oxford: Peter Lang, 2018).

Gordon, Stuart, 'Introduction', in Paul Kane and Marie O'Regan (eds.), *The Mammoth Book of Body Horror* (London: Robinson, 2012), pp. 1–5.

Grant, Michael, 'Body Horror', in Pam Cook (ed.), *The Cinema Book* (London: British Film Institute, 2007), pp. 355–60.

Haefele-Thomas, Ardel (ed.), *Queer Gothic: An Edinburgh Companion* (Edinburgh: Edinburgh University Press, 2023).

Hakin, Jamie, *Work that Body: Male Bodies in Digital Culture* (London: Rowman & Littlefield, 2020).

Halberstam, Jack J., *Skin Shows: Gothic Horror and the Technology of Monsters* (Durham: Duke University Press, 1995).

Hanich, Julian, *Cinematic Emotion in Horror Films and Thrillers: The Aesthetic Paradox of Pleasurable Fear* (New York: Routledge, 2010).

Haraway, Donna, 'The Biopolitics of Postmodern Bodies: Constitutions of Self in Immune System Discourse', *differences: A Journal of Feminist Cultural Studies* 1.1 (1989): 3–43.

Haraway, Donna, 'A Manifesto for Cyborgs: Science, Technology, and Socialist Feminism in the 1980s', *Socialist Review* 80 (1985): 65–108.

Hardt, Michael, and Antonio Negri, *Empire* (Cambridge: Harvard University Press, 2001 [2000]).

Harms, Eve, *Transmuted* (Power River: Unnerving, 2022).

Harrington, Erin, *Women, Monstrosity and Horror Film: Gynaehorror* (New York: Routledge, 2016).

Heron-Langton, Jessica, 'People Are Getting Surgery Younger than Ever Before: Is Social Media Really the Cause?' *Dazed*, 29 March 2019, www .dazeddigital.com/beauty/article/43837/1/surgery-youth-young-people-social-media [last accessed 16 November 2023].

Herzberg, David, *White Market Drugs: Big Pharma and the Hidden History of Addiction in America* (Chicago: The University of Chicago Press, 2020).

Huckvale, David, *The Philosophy of Body Horror in Film* (Jefferson: McFarland, 2020).

Hurley, Kelly, *The Gothic Body: Sexuality, Materialism, and Degeneration at the Fin de Siècle* (Cambridge: Cambridge University Press, 1996).

Huxley, Julian, *New Bottles for New Wine: Essays* (London: Chatto and Windus, 1957).

Jameson, Fredric, *The Cultural Turn: Selected Writings on the Postmodern, 1983–1998* (London: Verso, 2009 [1998]).

Jameson, Fredric, *Postmodernism, or, the Cultural Logic of Late Capitalism* (London: Verso, 1991).

Kato, Brooke, 'Gen Z Plastic Surgery Craze Hits All-Time High: I Want to "Feel Pretty Again"', *New York Post*, 21 February 2023, https://nypost.com/2023/02/20/plastic-surgeons-report-spike-in-gen-z-cosmetic-procedures/ [last accessed 16 November 2023].

Keetley, Dawn (ed.), *Get Out: Political Horror* (Columbus: Ohio State University Press, 2020).

Kendrick, James, *Hollywood Bloodshed: Violence in 1980s American Cinema* (Carbondale: Southern Illinois University Press, 2009).

Kilgour, Maggie, 'The Function of Cannibalism at the Present Time', in Francis Barker, Peter Hulme and Margaret Iversen (eds.), *Cannibalism and the Colonial World* (Cambridge: Cambridge University Press, 1998), pp. 238–59.

Krämer, Peter, *The New Hollywood: From Bonnie and Clyde to Star Wars* (London: Wallflower, 2005).

Kristeva, Julia, *Powers of Horror: An Essay on Abjection* (New York: Columbia University Press, 1982 [1980]).

Laine, Tarja, *Reframing Trauma in Contemporary Fiction Film* (Lanham: Lexington Books, 2023).

LaRocca, Eric, *Things Have Gotten Worse Since We Last Spoke and Other Misfortunes* (London: Titan, 2022).

Law, Tara, 'The Climate Crisis Is Global, but These 6 Places Face the Most Severe Consequences', *Time*, 30 September 2019, https://time.com/5687470/cities-countries-most-affected-by-climate-change/ [last accessed 7 November 2023].

LePan, Don, *Animals* (New York: Soft Skull Press, 2010 [2009]).

Lindsay, Cecile, 'Lyotard and the Postmodern Body', *L'Esprit Créateur* 31.1 (1991): 33–47.

López Cruz, Ronald Allan, 'Mutations and Metamorphoses: Body Horror Is Biological Horror', *Journal of Popular Film and Television* 40.4 (2012): 160–68.

Lovecraft, H. P., 'The Call of Cthulhu', *Weird Tales*, February (1928): 159–78.

Lowenstein, Adam, *Horror Film and Otherness* (New York: Columbia University Press, 2022).

Luckhurst, Roger, *Gothic: An Illustrated History* (London: Thames & Hudson, 2021).

Marche, Stephen, 'The Crisis of Intimacy in the Age of Digital Connectivity', *Los Angeles Review of Books*, 15 October 2018, https://lareviewofbooks.org/article/crisis-intimacy-age-digital-connectivity/ [last accessed 6 February 2024].

Mbembe, Achille, 'Necropolitics', *Public Culture* 15.1 (2003): 11–40.

McCluney, Courtney L., Kathrina Robotham, Serenity Lee, Richard Smith and Myles Durkee, 'The Costs of Code Switching', *Harvard Business Review*, 15 November 2019, https://hbr.org/2019/11/the-costs-of-codeswitching [last accessed 19 February 2024].

McHale, Brian, *Constructing Postmodernism* (New York: Routledge, 1992).

McLuhan, Marshall, *Understanding Media* (New York: Routledge, 2001 [1964]).

Morgan, Jack, *The Biology of Horror: Gothic Literature and Film* (Carbondale: Southern Illinois University Press, 2002).

Mulvey-Roberts, Marie, *Dangerous Bodies*: *Historicising the Gothic Corporeal* (Manchester: Manchester University Press, 2016).

Ndow, Gibril, J. Radeino Ambe and Oyewale Tomori, 'Emerging Infectious Diseases: A Historical and Scientific Review', in Godfrey B. Tangwa, Akin Abayomi, Samuel J. Ujewe and Nchangwi Syntia Munung (eds.), *Socio-cultural Dimensions of Emerging Diseases in Africa*: *An Indigenous Response to Deadly Epidemics* (Cham: Springer, 2019), pp. 31–40.

Oates, Joyce Carol, 'Introduction', in Joyce Carol Oates (ed.), *A Darker Shade*: *New Stories of Body Horror from Women Writers* (London: Footnote, 2023), pp. 1–7.

Okoth, Christine, 'The Black Body and the Reading of Race', in Travis M. Foster (ed.), *The Cambridge Companion to American Literature and the Body* (Cambridge: Cambridge University Press, 2022), pp. 227–41.

Olivier, Marc, 'Postdigital Gothic', in Catherine Spooner and Dale Townshend (eds.), *The Cambridge History of the Gothic*: *Volume 3. Gothic in the Twentieth and Twenty-First Centuries* (Cambridge: Cambridge University Press, 2021), pp. 323–41.

Ollett, Robyn, *The New Queer Gothic*: *Reading Queer Girls and Women in Contemporary Fiction and Film* (Cardiff: University of Wales Press, 2024).

Paul, William, *Laughing Screaming*: *Modern Hollywood Horror and Comedy* (New York: Columbia University Press, 1994).

Pearce, Ruth, Sonja Erikainen and Ben Vincent, 'TERF Wars: An Introduction', *The Sociological Review Monographs* 68.4 (2020): 677–98.

Peele, Jordan, 'Foreword', in Jordan Peele and John Joseph Adams (eds.), *Out There Screaming*: *An Anthology of New Black Horror* (London: Picador, 2023), pp. vii–viii.

Piatti-Farnell, Lorna, *Consuming Gothic*: *Food and Horror in Film* (Basingstoke: Palgrave Macmillan, 2017).

Pinker, Steven, 'The Mystery of Consciousness', *Time* 169.5 (2007): 58–62, 65–6, 69–70.

Piper, Hailey, *Queen of Teeth* (n.p.: Strangehouse Books, 2021).

Preciado, Paul B., *An Apartment in Uranus*, trans. Charlotte Mandell (London: Fitzcarraldo Editions, 2023a [2019]).

Preciado, Paul B., *Can the Monster Speak? A Report to an Academy of Psychoanalysts*, trans. Frank Wynne (London: Fitzcarraldo Editions, 2023b [2020]).

Preciado, Paul B., *Dysphoria Mundi: El sonido del mundo derrumbándonse* (Barcelona: Anagrama, 2022).

Priest, Hannah, 'Introduction: A History of Female Werewolves', in Hannah Priest (ed.), *She-Wolf: A Cultural History of Female Werewolves* (Manchester: Manchester University Press, 2015), pp. 1–23.

Quiggin, John, *Zombie Economics: How Dead Ideas Still Walk among Us* (Princeton: Princeton University Press, 2010).

Richardson, Niall, and Adam Locks, *Body Studies: The Basics* (New York: Routledge, 2014).

Roush, Ty, 'Hormone Therapy Lessened Depression: Lowered Suicide Risk among Transgender Adults, Study Says', *Forbes*, 7 September 2023, www .forbes.com/sites/tylerroush/2023/09/07/hormone-therapy-lessened-depres sion-lowered-suicide-risk-among-transgender-adults-study-says/?sh=122e f8ac4808 [last accessed 8 February 2024].

Ruff, Matt, *Lovecraft Country* (London: Picador, 2018 [2016]).

Rumfitt, Alison, *Brainwyrms* (London: Cipher Press, 2023).

Russell, Emily, *Transplant Fictions: A Cultural Study of Organ Exchange* (Cham: Palgrave Macmillan, 2019).

Russo, Mary, *The Female Grotesque: Risk, Excess and Modernity* (New York: Routledge, 1995 [1994]).

Sarup, Madan, *Identity, Culture and the Postmodern World* (Edinburgh: Edinburgh University Press, 1996).

Sawday, Jonathan, *The Body Emblazoned: Dissection and the Human Body in Renaissance Culture* (New York: Routledge, 1996).

Serano, Julia, *Whipping Girl: A Transsexual Woman on Sexism and the Scapegoating of Femininity*, 2nd ed. (New York: Seal Press, 2016 [2007]).

Shapiro, Stephen, 'Un-noveling *Lovecraft Country*', *Post45*, Arin Keeble and Samuel Thomas (eds.), 'New Literary Television' online cluster, 2 November 2021, https://post45.org/2021/11/un-noveling-lovecraft-country/ [last accessed 19 February 2024].

Shaviro, Steven, *The Cinematic Body* (Minneapolis: University of Minnesota Press, 1993).

Short, Sue, *Misfit Sisters: Screen Horror as Female Rites of Passage* (Basingstoke: Palgrave Macmillan, 2006), pp. 88–110.

Smith, Angela M., *Hideous Progeny: Disability, Eugenics, and Classic Horror Cinema* (New York: Columbia University Press, 2011).

Song, Jade, *Chlorine* (London: Footnote, 2023).

Spooner, Catherine, *Post-Millennial Gothic: Comedy, Romance and the Rise of Happy Gothic* (London: Bloomsbury, 2017).

Srnicek, Nick, *Platform Capitalism* (Cambridge: Polity, 2017).

Steven, Mark, *Splatter Capital: The Political Economy of Gore Films* (London: Repeater, 2017).

Taylor, Charles, *A Secular Age* (Cambridge: Harvard University Press, 2007).

Tudor, Andrew, 'Unruly Bodies, Unquiet Minds', *Body & Society* 1 (1993): 25–41.

Vallance, Chris, 'Artificial Intelligence Could Lead to Extinction, Experts Warn', *BBC News*, 30 May 2023, www.bbc.co.uk/news/uk-65746524 [last accessed 14 November 2023].

Verran, Jo, and Xavier Aldana Reyes, 'Emerging Infectious Literatures and the Zombie Condition', *Emerging Infectious Diseases* 24.9 (2018): 1774–78.

Voorhees, Roxie, and Nico Bell (eds.), *Mine: An Anthology of Body Autonomy Horror* (Brooklyn: Creature, 2022).

Wald, Priscilla, *Contagious: Cultures, Carriers, and the Outbreak Narrative* (Durham: Duke University Press, 2008).

Wasson, Sara, *Transplantation Gothic: Tissue Transfer in Literature, Film, and Medicine* (Manchester: Manchester University Press, 2020).

Webb, Jen, and Samuel Byrnand, 'Some Kind of Virus: The Zombie as Body and as Trope', *Body & Society* 14.2 (2008): 83–98.

Westengard, Laura, *Gothic Queer Culture: Marginalized Communities and the Ghosts of Insidious Trauma* (Lincoln: University of Nebraska Press, 2019).

Wester, Maisha, 'Black Lives Matter (BLM) Horror', in Simon Bacon (ed.), *The Evolution of Horror in the Twenty-First Century* (Lanham: Lexington Books, 2023), pp. 171–83.

Williams, Linda Ruth, 'A Virus Is Only Doing Its Job: From the Aliens Outside to Rebellion in the Flesh', *Sight and Sound* 31 (May 1993): 31–35.

Wolfe, Cary, *Before the Law: Humans and Other Animals in a Biopolitical Frame* (Chicago: The University of Chicago Press, 2013).

Wood, Robin, 'An Introduction to the American Horror Film', in Robin Wood and Richard Lippe (eds.), *American Nightmare: Essays on the Horror Film* (Toronto: Festival of Festivals, 1979), pp. 7–28.

Woodroe, Alex, and Matt Blairstone (eds.), *Your Body Is Not Your Body: A New Weird Horror Anthology* (Portland: Tenebrous Press, 2022).

Yoder, Rachel, *Nightbitch* (London: Vintage, 2022 [2021]).

Zuboff, Shoshana, *The Age of Surveillance Capitalism: The Fight for a Human Future at the New Frontier of Power* (London: Profile Books, 2019).

Acknowledgements

I wrote my first book, *Body Gothic*, with the strong conviction that body horror carries out important cultural work. Since its publication in 2014, a new wave of body horror has not just moved the subgenre into the mainstream but made it practically inescapable. What started in my mind as a conceptual afterword soon grew into a substantial and separate study. I would like to express my gratitude to Professors Dale Townshend and Angela Wright for their support and for encouraging me to bring this project to the Elements in the Gothic series. The editorial team at Cambridge University Press have also been fantastically helpful in materialising my vision for the book. I am particularly indebted to Julia Ford and George Paul Laver for their assistance with several procedural questions. The manuscript reviews were incredibly uplifting and reminded me why I feel compelled to research and write. I hugely appreciate the labour and feedback of these anonymous reviewers.

I would like to thank Manchester Metropolitan University, especially the Faculty of Arts and Humanities and the English department, for the period of sabbatical leave that allowed me to complete this book. Thanks also to Maisha Wester, Neil McRobert and Lexi Webster for their advice and suggestions, virtually all of which made it to the final text.

And as ever, thanks to my partner, family and friends for their love, patience and understanding. I would be a zombie husk without them.

I would like to dedicate this book to Miryam Aguilera Sosa.
Mil gracias por esas tardes de huldufólk, *tentáculos parlantes y trenes*
de carne de medianoche. Distantes, pero nunca olvidadas.

Cambridge Elements ☰

The Gothic

Dale Townshend
Manchester Metropolitan University
Dale Townshend is Professor of Gothic Literature in the Manchester Centre for Gothic Studies, Manchester Metropolitan University.

Angela Wright
University of Sheffield
Angela Wright is Professor of Romantic Literature in the School of English at the University of Sheffield and co-director of its Centre for the History of the Gothic.

Advisory Board

About the Series
Seeking to publish short, research-led yet accessible studies of the foundational 'elements' within Gothic Studies as well as showcasing new and emergent lines of scholarly enquiry, this innovative series brings to a range of specialist and non-specialist readers some of the most exciting developments in recent Gothic scholarship.

Cambridge Elements ☰

The Gothic

Printed in the United States
by Baker & Taylor Publisher Services